DATE DUE

D1518890

THE WORLD'S RAILROADS

FREIGHT BY RAIL

THE WORLD'S RAILROADS
FREIGHT BY RAIL

By Christopher Chant; edited by John Moore

Chelsea House Publishers
Philadelphia

Published in 2000 by
Chelsea House Publishers
1974 Sproul Road, Suite 400
P.O. Box 914
Broomall, PA 19008-0914

ISBN 0-7910-5562-0

Printed in China

Library of Congress Cataloging-in-Publication Data
Christopher Chant.
Freight by Rail / by Christopher Chant ; edited by John
Moore.
   p. cm. –(The World's Railroads)
Originally published: London : Regency House Pub.
Summary: Looks at the freight trains which are
responsible for hauling cargo all over the world.
   1. Railroads–Trains–Juvenile literature. 2. Railroads–
Freight-cars–Juvenile literature.
[1. Railroads–Trains.] I. Moore, John. II. Title. III Series.
TF148.C4544 1999
385'.37–dc21

                                                99-052632

TITLE PAGES: *A Chai He forestry
railway's 0-8-0, transporting a log train
towards a river bridge in China.*

OPPOSITE: *Union Pacific's Big Boy-class
simple-articulated 4-8-8-4 locomotive
No. 4023, the type first having been built in
1941.*

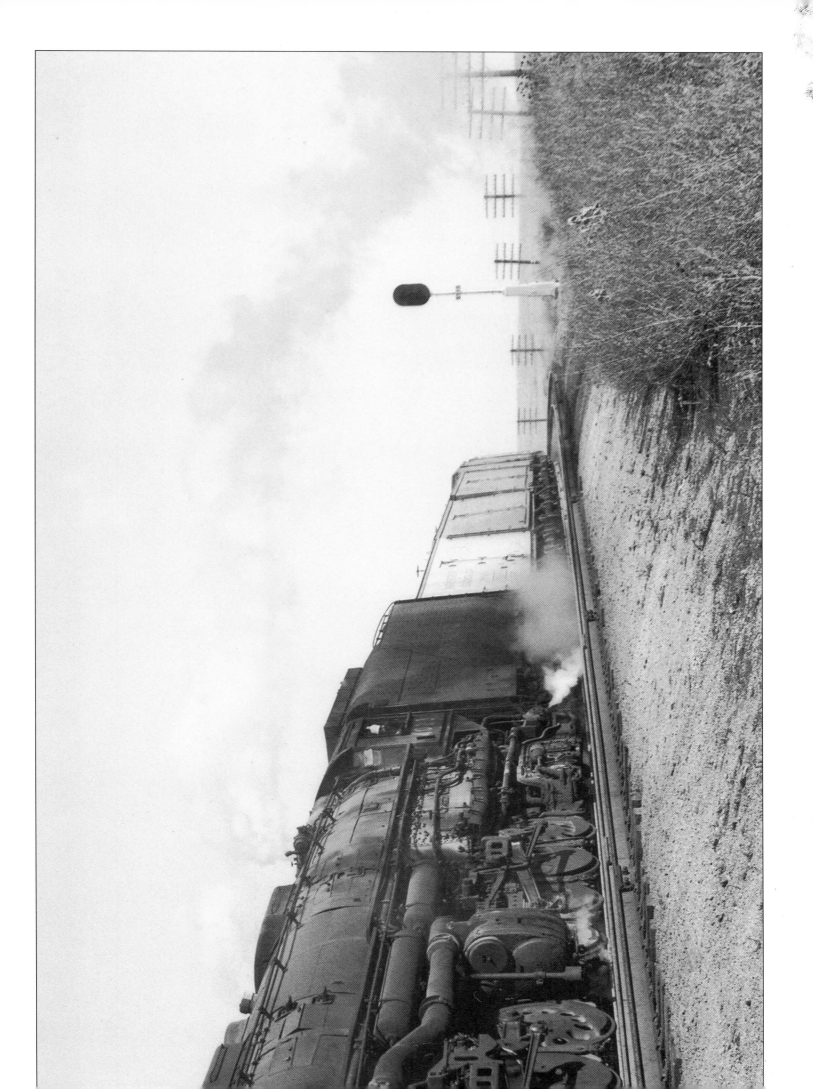

FREIGHT BY RAIL

Although the movement of freight, in the widest sense of the word, had been the driving force behind the creation of the first steam railroads, which served mining sites, it was the design and manufacture of the *Royal George* locomotive for the Stockton & Darlington Railway that signalled a new start in the development of the steam locomotive. Designed by Timothy Hackworth in 1827, the *Royal George* was the first 0-6-0 steam locomotive to be built for the mixed-traffic role, and as such the engine inaugurated the emergence of an entirely new type of locomotive that would, early in the 20th century, then evolve into the definitive type of heavy freight locomotive.

During the main period of the Victorian age there were two main types of steam locomotive, optimized for the hauling of passenger and freight trains. In the earlier part of the railroad age, the passenger locomotive was generally of the 0-4-2 or 2-4-0 layout, while the freight locomotive (or, as it was often called at the time, the baggage locomotive) was generally a tank or tender engine of the 0-6-0 configuration. By the 1880s most British and an increasing number of European railway and railroad companies were creating and using larger

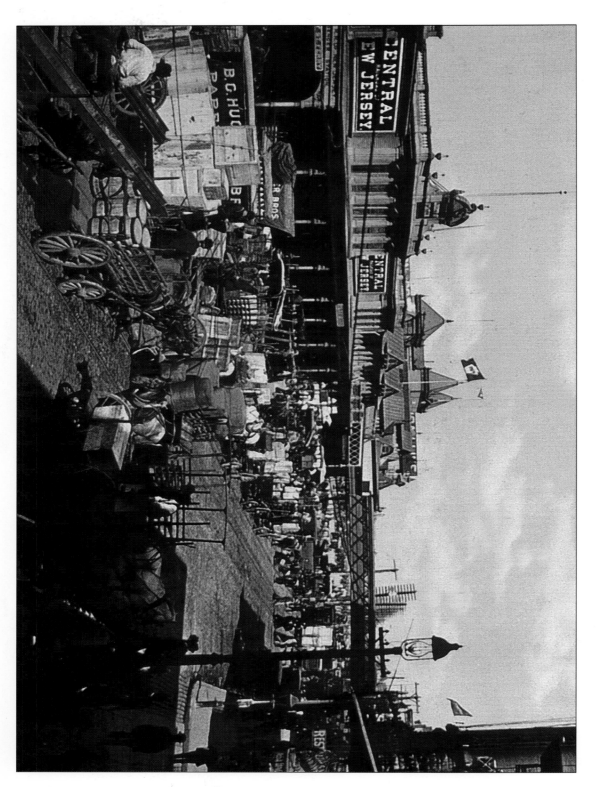

6

0-6-0 freight locomotives and indeed undertaking their first experiments with 0-8-0 locomotives for the hauling of heavy freight trains. In the United States, on the other hand, longer trains were the norm, and the designers and builders of steam locomotives were creating somewhat larger and heavier engines of the 2-6-0 and 2-8-0 layout for the hauling of heavy freight. These locomotives, of the bar-frame construction favoured by the Americans, were well suited to the comparatively rough country and poor track of the early U.S. railroads, and were also manufactured in significant numbers for export to South America, Australia and New Zealand, all of them regions in which conditions similar to those of the U.S.A. prevailed and therefore suggested the adoption of the American rather than European 'solution' to their railroad requirements.

As the 19th century progressed, and the weight of goods carried by freight trains grew steadily but remarkably, many European railways and North American railroads were, by the turn of the century, already starting to consider more effective means of hauling their heavy freight trains, now tasked with the movement not only of

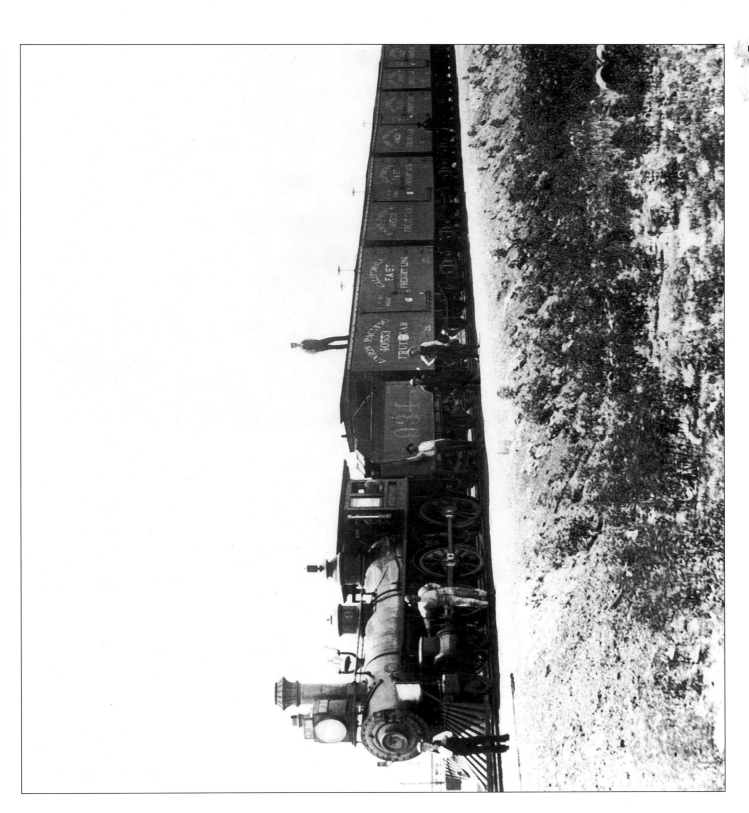

OPPOSITE: Depot of the Central Railroad, New Jersey, late 1800s.

RIGHT: Union Pacific locomotive 934 heads a block fruit train (before refrigerated cars were developed) in Nebraska, circa 1890.

ever increasing volumes of freight but also considerably heavier bulk loads such as coal and the raw materials required to feed the industries typical of the ever more industrialized Western nations. It was immediately clear that the current types of freight-optimized steam locomotives were inadequate for the task of hauling the longer and heavier trains that were now urgently demanded. In Europe, this led to the production of significantly heavier freight-hauling and switching locomotives, characterized by their 0-8-0, 0-10-0 and 2-10-0 layouts.

In Germany and Austria, very notably, a number of classes of standard locomotives evolved for this specific purpose, and one of the most important of the designers involved in such work was an Austro-Hungarian citizen, Karl Gölsdorf. Within the total of some 45 locomotive designs with which this talented engineer was credited, Gölsdorf created several classes of successful 2-8-0 and 2-10-0 heavy freight locomotives that were not only used within the Austro-Hungarian empire, but also exported in numbers to other countries in Europe, including as a particularly notable example Greece, whose state railroad system operated freight services using a large fleet of 2-8-0 and 2-10-0 locomotives imported from Austria-Hungary.

In Germany, the Royal Prussian state railroad system designed a number of standard classes of heavy freight locomotive based on the extensive use of common but well proven parts for maximum economy of manufacture and maintenance in combination with the highest possible level of reliability. These locomotives included the units of the 'G8' 0-8-0, 'G10' 0-10-0 and '44' classes, which were still in minor production when the various German railways were amalgamated into the nationalized Deutsche Reichsbahn in 1922.

Like their Austro-Hungarian cousins, these German standard designs were also exported in large numbers to other European railroad organizations, including those of Bulgaria, Poland, Romania and Turkey that all had strong economic and/or strategic ties with Germany.

In the initial absence of any significant national industrial and engineering capability, the development of railroads in Russia, from the 1830s, required that locomotives and other equipment of foreign designs, mainly from Germany and the U.K., be imported to provide an initial capability. Operation of these imported engines then provided the initial advantage of the earliest possible development and use of a railroad network, and at the same time the development of the operational experience that then allowed Russian steam locomotive designers to start producing effective engine designs, albeit with a strong British or German influence clearly evident, for domestic manufacture. Plants for the manufacture of all types of railroad equipment, using capital raised at home and also from abroad, were soon established to build all types of railroad equipment including locomotives that were better suited than imported engines to the particular geographic and climatic conditions in which the Russian railroads operated but which, as noted above, often displayed strong British and German design influences and also, to a slightly later and somewhat lesser extent, elements of American practice. The American influence grew as the Russian railroad system

expanded from the core region of western Russia into the less civilized outer reaches of the tsarist empire, where conditions more closely approximated those of the U.S.A. as its railroads expanded across North America. The need to construct large numbers of standard passenger and freight locomotives, together with the ever increasing length and weight of trains required for the movement of larger numbers of passengers and greater quantities of freight, heralded the production of the 'O' class of standard 0-8-0 locomotives. This locomotive, designed in the tsarist period, was so successful that, with only minor modifications, it was built by Russian

locomotive manufacturing plants right into the first two decades of the 20th century.

It should not be imagined that the development of an indigenous Russian locomotive designing and manufacturing capability meant that the various private and state-owned railroad organizations came to rely wholly on locomotives of Russian origin. Right up to the revolution of November 1917, which resulted in the establishment of the U.S.S.R. under a communist leadership with wholly different political, economic and social agendas, Russian railroad organizations were at various times buying and receiving large numbers of 0-8-0, 0-10-0 and, shortly before the outbreak of World War I in 1914,

2-10-0 steam locomotives from Germany and the U.S.A. By the 1920s the Soviet government had designed and manufactured several standard classes of locomotive for heavy freight use. These included the 'E' and 'FD' classes of 0-10-0 and 2-10-2 locomotives, to supplement the American-built Baldwin and Alco 2-10-0 locomotives supplied to Russia during World War I.

The relationship of the FD class with other Soviet locomotives of the period is an interesting aspect of how the U.S.S.R. was generally content, having found an acceptable industrial solution to a perceived economic requirement, to keep the resulting artefact in production and service without consideration of any real concept of

OPPOSITE: Freight being transferred from a Missouri river steamer to a Northern Pacific locomotive, North Dakota, 1880.

ABOVE LEFT: A snow-clearing gang and equipment near Stampede, 1886.

ABOVE: Railroads played a key role in the industrial and agricultural development of the United States. This picture, from the late 19th century, shows freight cars loaded with cotton in St. Louis, Missouri railroad yards.

'modernization': if a locomotive was technically successful in meeting state needs and was cheap both to build and to operate, it was kept in production and service in its original form and also in any variants that could readily be derived from it. Thus, when by 1930 it had created the very effective 'S' class of passenger locomotives, of which some 3,000 were built for long-term service without any 'consumer' pressure for radical improvement, the Soviet authorities could take their time in assessing the longer-term needs of a growing requirement for passenger transport, which up to this time had been secondary in Soviet thinking to the demands for the freight transport on which the much-desired industrialization of the Soviet state was heavily dependent. It was now appreciated that higher speeds and

more comfortable (thus weightier) trains would eventually be needed.

The first prototype of the new generation of locomotive appeared during 1932 as what was really little more than an expansion of the 2-6-2 S-class design into a 2-8-4 layout with an additional coupled axle for more tractive effort, and also an additional carrying axle at the rear to allow the incorporation of a larger firebox so that the engine could generate more power for the use of the improved motive system. The design was designated as the 'IS' class in honour of the Soviet leader, Iosef Stalin, and some 640 such locomotives were manufacturing in the period between 1934 and the time of the German invasion of the U.S.S.R. in 1941. The type has disappeared from service in its original passenger train version, but a derived freight version (with

ABOVE LEFT: The Italian locomotive Le Rubican on the Porrettana mountain line, 1863.

ABOVE: The Breda works with employees and locomotives, Italy 1892. By the end of the 19th century in Europe, the weight of goods carried had grown significantly, requiring more powerful locomotives.

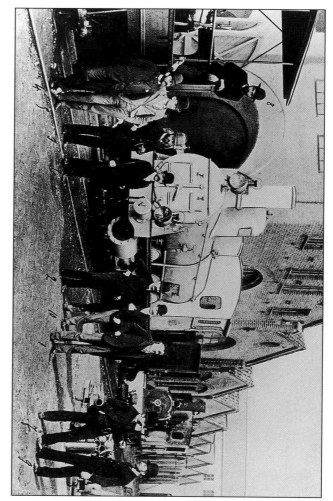

the same boiler, cab, cylinders, tender and other parts) is the FD class of 2-10-2 locomotive, of which substantial numbers are in use throughout southern China, after being adapted to standard gauge from the Russian 5ft 0in (1.524m) gauge.

The production of closely related passenger and freight locomotives was of course typical of the Soviet authorities' approach, both financially sensible and technically logical, toward the needs of the state railroad system. To this extent, therefore, the Soviet regime differed only marginally from the tsarist system it replaced. Also typical of the Soviet system, however, was the manufacture in 1937 and 1938 of the first three of a planned total of 10 streamlined 4-6-4 locomotives to haul the high-speed Red Arrow express between Moscow and Leningrad, a journey of

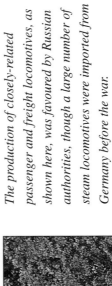

The production of closely-related passenger and freight locomotives, as shown here, was favoured by Russian authorities, though a large number of steam locomotives were imported from Germany before the war.

slightly more than 401 miles (645km) on which an average speed of 40.5 to 50mph (65 to 80km/h) was planned. The initial pair of locomotives each had driving wheels with a diameter of 6ft 6.75in (2.00m) but the third unit had driving wheels with a diameter of 7ft 2.5in (2.197m). All three of the locomotives were based in design and mechanical detail on the FD class, with which they shared the boilers, cylinders and much else. The German invasion prevented the construction of the last seven of the locomotives, but initial service had revealed the class to have excellent performance including a maximum speed of 106mph (170km/h).

The ever increasing weight and length of passenger and freight trains had made it clear by the end of the 19th century, at least

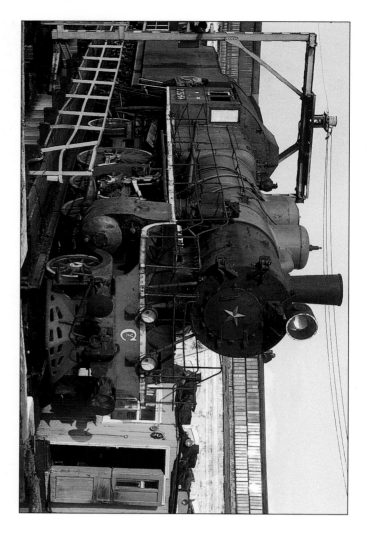

to the larger and more far-sighted railroad organizations, that the continued success of steam-powered railroad services in all but the flattest and smallest countries demanded the introduction of either larger and more powerful locomotives or of banking, or 'helper', locomotives to ease heavy trains over hilly country. The former was clearly the simpler solution but meant that much of the new locomotives' power would be unnecessary for the more level and less demanding majority of the railroad network, while the latter meant the adoption of new locomotives that could be reserved for use as ancillaries only on the steeper gradients where the standard main-line locomotives actually needed their assistance. For many decades the larger railway companies had been using conventional 4-4-0 and 0-6-0

locomotives for this banking purpose, and had found the concept adequate to their needs. By the late 1880s, however, it had started to become abundantly clear that the demands of banking what had become considerably longer and heavier trains, with further increases inevitable, demanded the use of more powerful (and therefore larger) banking locomotives.

Returning to the subject of banking engines, the British-administered railroads of India also faced problems in the first part of the 20th century similar to those encountered in North America. The need to bank trains over steeper gradients required the design and manufacture of a class of heavy tank locomotive built to the 0-8-4T arrangement. These locomotives, along with some 2-8-4T engines, were used on the Ghat

incline of the Great Indian Peninsula Railway.

South African railways were quick to appreciate the importance of powerful banking locomotives. Shortly before World War I, therefore, they ordered a batch of Mallet-type locomotives from North British of Glasgow. These machines were used on heavy freight and banking duties until the early 1950s, when they were withdrawn. New Zealand railways also needed a solution to the difficulty of moving large passenger and freight trains over difficult terrain. Rather than adopt the banking engine solution, however, the New Zealanders decided to approach the problem from a different angle and opted for the construction of an incline railroad using the Fell system of braking, which required the

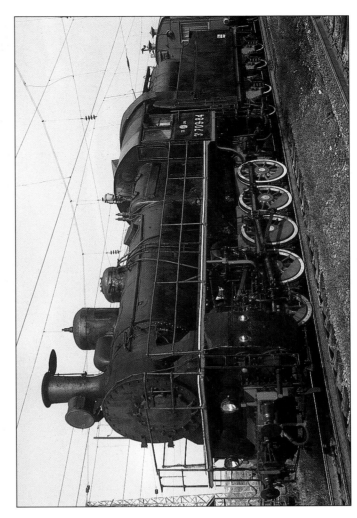

ABOVE: The ever-increasing weight of freight carried required more powerful or 'helper' locomotives in all but the flattest terrain.

RIGHT: Two examples of Russian steam power.

OPPOSITE
LEFT: The Russian S class was a standard-design locomotive used by many independent railways before the Russian Revolution.

RIGHT: Russian Su-class 2-6-2 locomotive, of which more than 2,000 were built in 15 years. The 'S' stood for the Soromovo works where the class was built, and the 'u' for usilennyi, which means 'strengthened'.

manufacture of specially designed 0-4-2 tank locomotives. The Fell braking system worked from a central rail that retarded the locomotive and train working on railroad lines with a steep gradient: this frequently required the use of several locomotives working together, depending on the weight of the train being banked.

Possibly the first North American railroad to appreciate the problem of banking locomotives was the Baltimore & Ohio Railroad. In 1904 this organization felt that it had started to arrive at the right solution to the problem, and therefore manufactured the first American example of the kind of banking locomotive developed by Anatole Mallet as a type with two sets of coupled wheels, of which the first set was

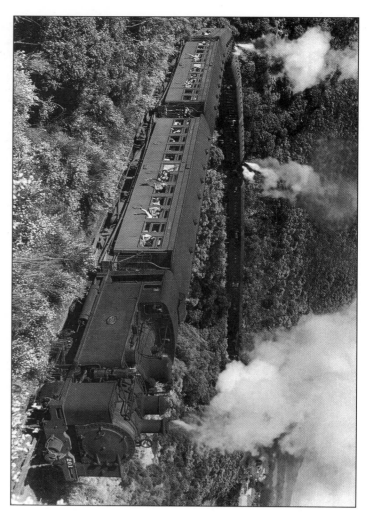

pivoted to become a motor bogie or truck, in the process turning the Mallet type of locomotive into a semi-articulated unit. The Baltimore & Ohio Railroad's Mallet-type locomotive, nicknamed *Old Maud*, was used for experiments in the banking of heavy trains over long and twisting gradients that otherwise required the use of multiple-heading of locomotives. *Old Maud* proved to be eminently useful and, in the years that followed, most of the larger railroad operators in North America either built in their own plants or ordered from specialist locomotive manufacturers Mallet locomotives of the same basic type or alternatively more conventional 2-8-0 or 2-10-0 locomotives to bank heavy trains up steeper gradients.

OPPOSITE
LEFT: The Rimutuka incline near Wellington on the North Island of New Zealand where several engines were interspersed along the train to climb the steep incline using the Fell system of braking.

RIGHT: Soviet P36 – the epitome of Russian steam locomotives – with cab totally enclosed against the Russian winter.

THIS PAGE
LEFT: The Soviet P36 class was originally designed for passenger service but was subsequently used for hauling heavy freight.

BELOW: Name plate of a P36 locomotive.

In the U.K. the Midland Railway constructed a 0-10-0 tender locomotive which also had a nickname, in this instance *Big Emma* or sometimes *Big Bertha*. Manufactured in 1919, just after the end of World War I, this locomotive was used on the Lickey incline at Bromsgrove near Birmingham in the Midlands, where its success as a banking unit meant its retention up to 1956, when it was replaced by a British Railways '9F'-class 2-10-0 locomotive. At much the same time, for the not altogether unrelated task of heavy hump-shunting in goods yards. These locomotives survived into the later part of the 1940s, in the process lasting long

enough to be taken into the stock of privately owned locomotives inherited by the nationalized British Railways organization. In 1925, the London & North Eastern Railway ordered a Beyer-Garratt locomotive for service on the Worsborough incline near Barnsley in Yorkshire. This 2-8-8-2 locomotive remained in service until the line was electrified in 1955, after which it was tried on the Lickey incline in company with *Big Bertha*, and was withdrawn only in 1956 when it was scrapped. In 1921 the London & South Western Railway ordered three examples of a 4-8-0 tank locomotive designed by Robert Urie, and these engines were employed at the new marshalling yard at Feltham on the edge of London to hump-shunt freight

wagons into formation. All three of the locomotives were withdrawn from service in 1962.

The Mallet type of semi-articulated locomotive had first appeared in the alpine regions of Europe from 1889 but found only a modest level of acceptance. As can be deduced from the above, however, the Americans were more chary even of evaluating the type and thus it was only in 1904 that J.E. Muhlfeld, Chief of Motive Power on the Baltimore & Ohio Railroad, thought that the type would also be useful for the hauling of very heavy coal trains and designed a huge double 0-6-0 (C-C) steam locomotive. This engine was immediately a great success, and the U.S. railroads soon adopted the Mallet type of

ABOVE: K-class locomotive K-8-c 2-8-0 (No. 2651) fitted with pilot snow plough at Rigby, Maine, 1939.

ABOVE RIGHT: A London & North Eastern Railway Garratt, hauling passenger coaches. Garratt, an Englishman who lived in Australia, invented this famous type of articulated locomotive.

RIGHT: Baltimore & Ohio Railroad's EM-1-class Mallet 2-8-8-4 No. 7600, newly arrived from Baldwin and ready to start work on the Cumberland Division, 1944.

LEFT: London & North Eastern Railway Garratt U1-class locomotive No. 2395. Articulated locomotives such as the Garratt got round the problems caused by very long-boilered locomotives on curves.

BELOW: Norfolk & Western Y6B Mallet No. 2142 (2-8-8-2) on an eastbound freight-train taking water at Relspring, Virginia.

locomotive in increasing numbers as bankers and prime movers for heavy freight trains. The Mallet type of locomotive was not characterized by any high level of performance, in terms of either speed or acceleration, but was very powerful indeed and also notably easy on the road. Thus the Mallet type of locomotive, which had started as a small double-0-4-0 tank engine, then matured in the U.S.A. as a heavy hauler of increasing size and power.

Thus the process started by Muhlfeld soon developed into a series of truly monstrous engines, of which perhaps the finest example was the *Matt H. Shay* of the Erie Railroad before World War I, which had two sets of coupled wheels, in each case comprising four axles, and a third essentially identical set under the tender to provide an overall 2-8-8-2 layout for what became known as the 'Triplex' configuration. There was nothing new in the

concept of the steam-powered tender, which had been manufactured and used by both the Ouest railroad in France and the Great Northern Railway in the U.K. during the middle part of the previous century, in both cases for additional traction during difficult moments such as starting and continued motion up steep gradients. The concept of the powered tender, in all of its forms, had a major problem, however, namely the relative shortage of steam for all the cylinders that had to be operated.

Another problem with the type of long locomotives that were introduced to provide greater tractive effort in the particular low-performance environment typical of freight operations was the very length of the boiler's barrel length that was now possible from the metallurgical and firing points of view, but which presented difficulties on railroad tracks with all but the gentlest of curves. As a result, there were many

attempts to create an effective type of articulated boiler, with two sections connected in the centre by a bellows arrangement, but the technical problems of such an arrangement were beyond effective solution. Among the railroads that sought to develop such a boiler was the Atchison, Topeka and Santa Fe, which produced a locomotive with six coupled axles in two sets, giving the unit a 2-6-6-2 layout at an overall weight of 689,920lb (312948kg), increased by a further 262,080lb (11879kg) by the 12-wheel tender. Fortunately for the crew, this monster was oil- rather than coal-fired!

The Mallet type of locomotive also made an appearance in several other parts of the world, although not on such a gigantic scale as in the United States, and also in generally smaller numbers. British locomotive manufacturing companies built such engines for operators in Burma, China and South Africa; several French railroad companies built and used the type on the railroad network of France; and in Germany the Maffei company produced Mallet-type locomotives for service with the Royal Bavarian state railroad, with the Royal Hungarian state railroad and also, in broad-gauge forms, with the Central Aragon and Zafra-Huelva railroads in Spain.

The U.K. was responsible for the creation of another classic type of articulated locomotive, which was so extensively and successfully operated in many parts of the world at a later date that the Americans, who in fact never adopted the type, came to call it the 'British Mallet',

even though its real name was the Beyer-Garratt, so named for its designer, Herbert Garratt who was an Englishman who lived in Australia and created the first such articulated locomotive in 1909, and Beyer, Peacock and Company that was based in Manchester and later bought Garratt's patents.

In basic terms the Beyer-Garratt consisted of two separate locomotive units that supported, by means of pivots and bearings, the proportionally large boiler carried on a girder frame between them. Garratt's original idea had been that this arrangement would allow the creation of a

large and powerful, yet flexible, passenger engine in which the dimensions of the boiler would not be limited by the height of the large-diameter driving wheels, as was the case with more conventional steam locomotives. Such a passenger locomotive, with a 2-4-0+0-4-2 wheel arrangement, was in fact manufactured for the São Paulo Railway of Brazil during 1915, but the very first of the type were a few small double 0-4-0 locomotives for very narrow gauges, typified by the singular 2ft 0in (0.61m) gauge of the Tasmanian Government Railway (1909) and for the Darjeeling Himalayan Railway in India (1911). The

OPPOSITE: The magnificent Beyer-Garratt locomotive, favourite for hauling freight in many parts of the world, particularly in Africa and Australia.

ABOVE LEFT: The basic Beyer-Garratt locomotive consists of two separate locomotive units which share a large common boiler.

ABOVE: Known to Americans as the 'British Mallet', the Beyer-Garratt locomotive had excellent riding and traction qualities.

19

Garratt locomotive therefore started life as an engine used almost exclusively on narrow-gauge railroads in mountainous regions, but soon developed into a massive type whose basic features generally included outside cylinders with Walschaert valve gear and, with the exception of the Tasmanian unit, simple rather than compound expansion.

The Beyer-Garratt was not the only type of articulated locomotive that saw service in the first quarter of the 20th century. There was also the Meyer type that first appeared in Belgium during 1873 with origins stretching to an earlier time: the Meyer type of locomotive had two motor bogies or trucks, with the leading unit on a spherical pivot and the trailing unit on a transverse members to carry one large boiler. The main frames were those of the two motor units, which therefore carried the couplers, and the boiler supported the tanks. It was only in the 1890s that the Meyer type of locomotive began to gain any real acceptance after the type was recommended to Kitson & Co. in the U.K. by Robert Stirling of the Anglo-Chilean Nitrate Company's railroad. In this British-developed model the boiler, tanks and bunker were installed on a pair of parallel girders whose ends rested on the bogies or trucks. Used for the movement of nitrates to the Chilean coast, the locomotives coped well with a 1/25 gradient of the 17-mile (27-km) route, of which a fair measure was also typified by curves of a moderately small radius. The same type of locomotive was used with considerable success on the

Argentine and Chilean narrow-gauge railroads across the Andes mountains and also, in a considerably broader gauge, on the ore-carrying routes of southern Spain.

Other articulated steam locomotives of the period included not only the original type of Fairlie but also the so-called Modified Fairlie and the Maffei-built Garratt Union, both owing much to the Garratt, and the Hagans which had two sets of coupled wheels and included drive to the rear set. The Hagans was manufactured for

the Royal Prussian state railroad in 1893, and also for the Tasmanian Government.

Despite the success of articulated steam locomotives (of which the Mallet type predominated in North America, the Garratt in Africa, the Meyer in South America, and the older Fairlie in Mexico) for the heavy freight role, the only one to secure additional success in the passenger locomotive role was the Garratt. And not even the levels of technical and commercial success attained by several of these

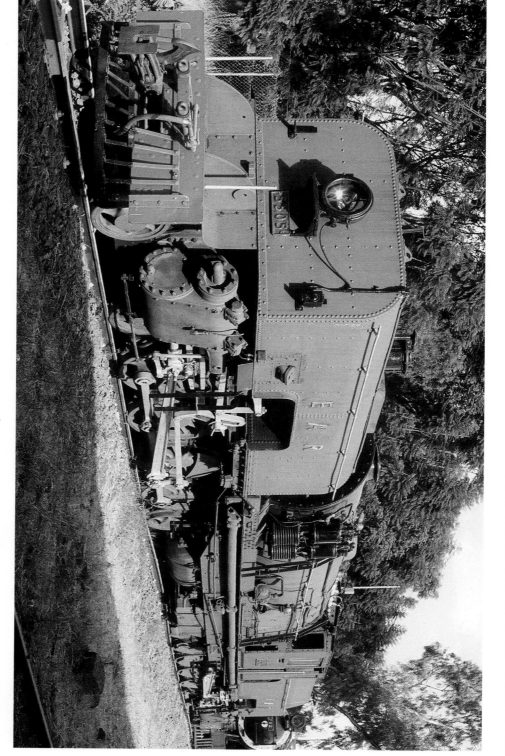

ABOVE: No. 5505 of the East African Railway, built by Beyer-Peacock in 1945 for Tanganyika Railway.

OPPOSITE: GMA Garratt No. 4165 shunts in factory sidings at Pietermaritzburg, South Africa. These locomotives were favourites for hauling freight in Africa.

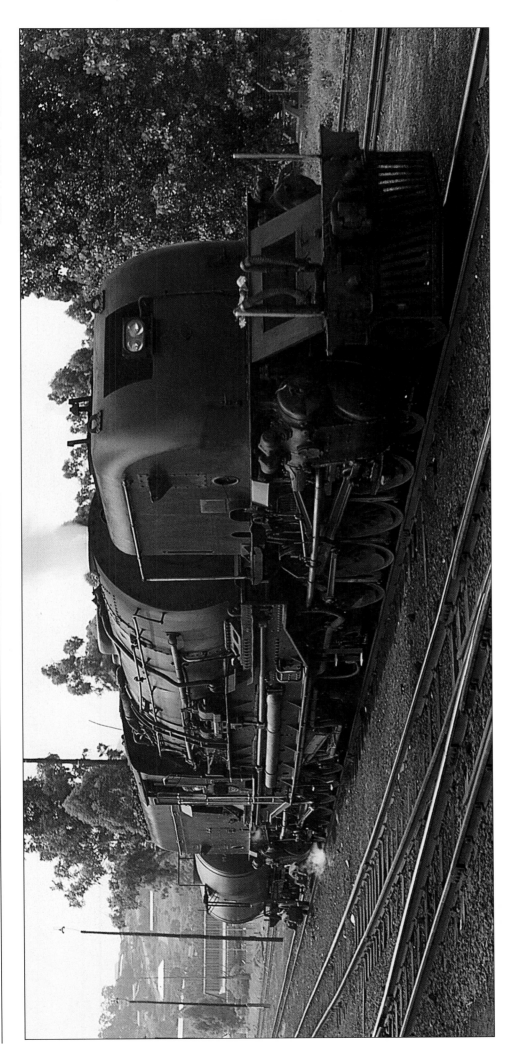

articulateds could convince all the world's railroad operators that there was real merit in the apparent complexity of these powerful locomotives. Thus many railroads placed their entire faith in the original type of steam locomotive with a rigid framework carried on the track by wheels on several axles and itself supporting the rest of the locomotive's apparatus. As noted above, the 0-10-0 locomotive was most favoured in central and eastern Europe in countries such as

Austria-Hungary, Germany (most notably Prussia and Bavaria), Italy, Sweden and, most significantly of all, Russia. In this last nation, an excellent design was introduced just before the outbreak of World War I, and this was eventually to be manufactured in numbers running into several thousands, especially as an all-purpose type in the immensely troubled period after the revolution of November 1917 had turned tsarist Russia into the communist U.S.S.R.: many of the locomotives were also

manufactured in Sweden by Nydqvist and Helm, and in Germany by companies such as Vulkan and Humboldt. Such was the basic simplicity and reliability of the design that few changes were ever needed, and the type served the U.S.S.R. long and faithfully.

In North America, the locomotive of 0-10-0 layout was used only as a heavy switcher in the great freight yards. For main-line freight-hauling operations, the Americans preferred the locomotive of the 2-10-2 type, whose bogies or trucks

provided a better ride on the road than any locomotive of the wholly rigid type. The locomotive of 2-10-0 layout was much appreciated in Europe, especially in Austria-Hungary and in the Balkans, where the type's success led to additional use for express passenger services, initially on routes such as the Semmering, Tauern and Arlberg railways in Austria before their electrification, and then in Greece. In this latter, engines of a patently Austro-Hungarian design origin, but manufactured by Skoda in Czechoslovakia after the break-up of the Habsburg empire, were even used on this section of the *Orient Express* route.

Though it did see a measure of passenger service, however, the locomotive of the 2-10-0 type was best suited to freight operations such as the hauling of heavy coal trains, and it was in this role that classic locomotives, such as the 2-10-0 type designed by J.D. Flamme for the Belgian state railroad in the 1920s, made their names. Other 2-10-0 locomotives were produced in Austria-Hungary (in many ways the archetypal parent of the large steam locomotive in Europe), but expansions of this core type included 2-12-0 locomotives produced in limited numbers in both Austria-Hungary and Württemberg, and then at a somewhat later date by France, where the 'A1' class of 2-12-0 locomotives was built for the nationalized railroad system from 1948.

For the purposes of hauling heavy freight trains, however, the locomotive with a long rigid wheelbase was in general inferior to the locomotive with articulated groupings of wheels, such as the Mallet and Garratt types. In overall terms, therefore, the very long coupled wheelbase did not survive long, even though the death throes of the type were extended by final experiments such as the classically huge 4-14-4 locomotive produced in the U.S.S.R. during 1934 for evaluation against an even more substantial Beyer-Garratt 4-8-2+2-8-4 locomotive obtained from the U.K. in the previous year. The fact that neither was repeated in a sure indication

that both the types were unsuccessful.

By the start of the 20th century, the development of the heavy freight locomotive in its basic but specialized role had reached an advanced stage. Quite apart from the use of 0-6-0, 0-8-0 and 2-8-0 engines as their primary locomotives for this task, many main-line railway companies were looking at alternative methods to overcome their operating problems. In the years up to 1914, the majority of British main-line companies had ordered or constructed some 2-8-0 freight locomotives. These included the Great Western Railway, which had a sizeable fleet of '2800'-class locomotives and nine '4700'-class large-wheeled 2-8-0 locomotives. The Great Northern Railway, under the technical supervision of Nigel Gresley, designed some successful standard 2-8-0 locomotives for heavy coal and freight traffic from the north-east of England to London. Perhaps the best known type of British heavy freight locomotive of the Edwardian era was the Robinson ROD (Railway Operating Division) 2-8-0 locomotive, many of which were constructed for use by the British army in World War I.

After the establishment of the London & North Eastern Railway in 1923 through the amalgamation of several smaller railway companies, Gresley designed the 'P1' class of 2-8-2 Mikado-type locomotives to undertake heavy freight work from London on what had recently been the Great Northern Railway's main line. These locomotives were, paradoxically, too

successful in technical terms as their considerable power meant that especial care had to be taken to avoid breaking the couplings of the small two-axle coal and goods wagons then in use. Arguably the best, and certainly the most successful type of locomotive ever designed in the U.K. for the heavy freight role, was Sir William Stanier's '8F'-class 2-8-0 unit, which was manufactured for the London, Midland & Scottish Railway in the period between 1937 and 1944. So successful was the type that the War Office also ordered many batches for its own purposes, which included operations in many parts of the world, especially in the Middle East and Persia (now Iran), where trains hauled by 8F-class locomotives were importantly operated to deliver allied war materiel to the forces and industries of the U.S.S.R. across Persia's northern frontier after the goods had reached the region by ship.

As noted above, in the more developed countries of the British empire, the problem of operating heavy freight was overcome by the use of both conventional and articulated locomotives. The development and adoption of the Beyer-Garratt locomotive after 1907 was particularly important for railroad operations in Africa, where the type proved to be a highly effective solution for some of the worst problems encountered by railway engineers and administrators. In South Africa, most notably, the Beyer-Garratt locomotives of the 'GL' and 'GMAM' classes were outstandingly effective in terms of performance and reliability, and their availability in significant numbers

successfully overcame many of the difficulties that had previously afflicted railroad operations in this important area.

By the 1880s, the main railroad operators in all parts of continental Europe, eastern, central and western, were heavily involved in the development, manufacture and large-scale introduction of locomotives of steadily increasing size and capability for the operation of heavy freight services and, to a somewhat lesser extent, mixed traffic operations. Among the first to come to a full appreciation of the benefits offered by such locomotives were several of the larger state railroad organizations of the German empire. When, in the aftermath of Germany's defeat in World War I, the new German republic decided to create a national railroad system by

OPPOSITE LEFT: American-style water columns can be turned off from the top of the tender.

RIGHT: EM-1 locomotive No. 7611 carrying coal at the highest point of the Baltimore & Ohio main-line system. At this point, near Altamont, Maryland, the trains come off the Deer Park grade and immediately drop down onto the Seventeen-Mile grade.

amalgamating the various private and state-owned railroads into the Deutsche Reichsbahn during 1922, the already existing process of developing and manufacturing standard classes, generally based on Prussian designs with a measure of input from the railroad practices of Bavaria and Württemberg, was expanded to include 2-8-0, 2-10-0 and 2-10-2T types of locomotives in large numbers. The French railroad operators had drawn major benefit from locomotive construction during World War I, and

also from the import of '140C'-class 2-8-0 and American-built 'Pershing'-type 2-8-0 locomotives. This process was repeated after World War II, when the Société Nationale des Chemins de Fer further benefited from the acquisition of '141R'-class 2-8-2 locomotives as part of the Marshall Plan designed by General George C. Marshall to help Europe recover its economic feet.

By a time early in the 20th century, the American railroad companies had developed a large network of services

operating, among other things, an increasing volume of the freight that represented, on the one hand, the raw materials needed for the rapidly continuing development of American industrialization and, on the other hand, finished goods for domestic consumption or for export from the country's large numbers of major sea ports. In this situation, the design, manufacture and deployment of the latest generation of efficient heavy locomotives to haul these freight trains was of huge importance. A number of the larger railroad companies themselves developed

locomotives to meet the need. The Union Pacific Railroad in particular produced two classes of locomotives of outstanding design. These were the 'Challenger' and the 'Big Boy'. Both types were developed from the late 1930s and construction continued until the late 1940s. The Big Boy, designed by Alco and built to the extent of 25 '4000'-class locomotives, can be regarded as one of the last, and therefore definitive types of huge steam locomotive for heavy freight haulage purposes. The details for these magnificent superheated locomotives included a 4-8-8-4 layout, four

LEFT: *British Black 8 2-8-0 with a mixed freight near Chippenham, Wiltshire.*

BELOW LEFT: *Type 11/12 locomotive used to haul freight on the Portuguese narrow-gauge lines.*

BELOW RIGHT *Portuguese state railway 2-2-2 locomotive. By the 1880s in Europe it was found that 0-6-0 and 0-8-0 locomotives were more suitable for freight operations.*

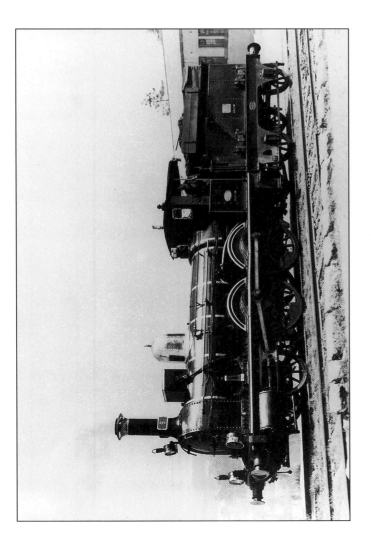

ABOVE LEFT: This early Portuguese state railway series 2-4-0 locomotive was more likely to have been used for mixed passenger-freight traffic.

ABOVE: Portuguese state railway 204 locomotive. Increasingly, heavy freight loads demanded larger locomotives.

LEFT: Garratt 742 No. 19, en route to Bulawayo, Zimbabwe.

23.75 x 32-in (603 x 813-mm) cylinders, steam pressure of 300lb/sq in (21.1kg/cm²), and a weight of 772,000lb (350179kg) excluding the tender, which turned the scales at 348,000lb (157853kg) at two-thirds maximum load.

They were the last heavy freight locomotives in service on the Union Pacific Railroad, and the locomotives were not withdrawn until 1959. The Norfolk & Western Railroad, which hauled heavy coal trains in Virginia, had a large fleet of 'Y6B'- and 'A'- class articulated locomotives of the Mallet type, and these too were notable for the superb service they provided from the early 1930s to 1960, when they were finally retired from service as the last steam locomotives used in the U.S.A. for the hauling of heavy freight trains.

Before turning to the introduction of the new motive technologies represented by diesel and electric power, of which the former was applied equally to passenger and freight trains, it is instructive to look at the types of specialized steam locomotives that were adopted for and are often still used for a number of secondary freight transport purposes. The aspect that comes most readily to mind is the movement of coal, which is a material that was at once the reason that steam railways and railroads could initially be created and at the same time one of the prime materials that required mass transport as the onset of the Industrial Revolution and urbanization created increasing demands for coal in areas both close to and distant from the coal

fields. At the smallest level of coal movement, by the mid-1800s the colliery railroad had become an intrinsic part of the industrial landscape, and a notable feature in the creation and operation of these individually small but collectively large networks was the constricted layout imposed on the colliery railroad by the nature of the coal mine it served, and this fact often made it impossible to use the type of medium- and large-sized locomotive typical of main-line service at the time, the type of locomotive most frequently encountered in the colliery railroad operations of the period being the 0-6-0T configuration.

A classic example of the definitive sort of colliery railroad was that located at Ashington in the north-east of England, which started work during 1850. Although initially restricted to services within the area of the coal mine, the colliery railroad was soon expanded to include a connection with the North Eastern Railway's main line at Blyth, which allowed the bulk movement of coal to local ports for export to countries such as Germany, Poland and Sweden. It is also worth noting that Ashington was also a main source for the so-called 'steam coal' that was moved by railroad to locomotive sheds all over the U.K. By the mid-1930s, the company possessed some 15 miles (24km) of track together with about 9 miles (14.5km) of sidings that provided storage for up to 35,000 tons of coal in wagons. The colliery railroad operated some 750 wagons that were hauled by a force of 17 small steam locomotives. Some of the

possible to use engines larger than those typical of European practice, generally up to the 4-8-2 types that provided an effective haulage capability on colliery railroad/main-line railroad connecting tracks which were more like branch lines in their own right. This concept was as true of Australia as South Africa, for the vast size of the country and the dispersed nature of its coal fields meant that the connections between the colliery railroad and main-line railroad were often worked by tender engines that had originally been operated for main-line services. In highly congested countries such as India, however, the most common gauge used for the coal fields in Assam and other areas was 2ft 0in (0.61m), and on this gauge there operated very small engines, generally of the saddle-tank type with an 0-4-0 or 0-1-2 layout. This was not exclusively the case, moreover, as attested by the use of a 5ft 6in (1.68m) gauge and main-line engines for the huge complex of mines around Asansol.

In the United States, the railroad lines serving coal-mining areas have been important right from the start of the industrial revolution in America, and at the industry's peak there were very many lines, mostly of the narrow-gauge type, extending below the surface of the ground to lift the coal to the surface from the underground galleries in which it was mined. Such operations were entirely typical of the coal-mining industry in key areas such as Colorado, Pennsylvania, Utah and West Virginia, whose vast coal deposits (combined with similarly huge deposits of

bigger collieries in the U.K. also ran passenger trains to coincide with the beginnings and ends of various shifts, thereby facilitating the movement of the miners between the pit head and the neighbouring villages in which most of them lived. These services generally made use of obsolete rolling stock bought from main-line operators, and as a result some of the trains were fascinating for their combination of miscellaneous coaches (of all classes) from main-line companies operating in all parts of the U.K. By the early part of the 20th century, there were some hundreds of collieries operating in the U.K., and many of these had their own railroads, but passenger services ended many years ago.

Although the U.K. had by far the most collieries, specialized railroad operations of this type were just as significant in the pattern of European coal and railroad development, especially in the Ruhr region of Germany, in Poland and in Russia, where the location and exploitation of large coal reserves were seen as an important milestone in the industrialization and economic development of the countries in question. As in the U.K., the geographical constraints on the coal-mining areas that were thus developed often imposed an upper limit on the size of the locomotives that could be employed, but in other parts of the world, most notably regions such as South Africa, where an effectively fresh start could be made and longer distances had to be covered before the colliery railroad could link with a main line, it was

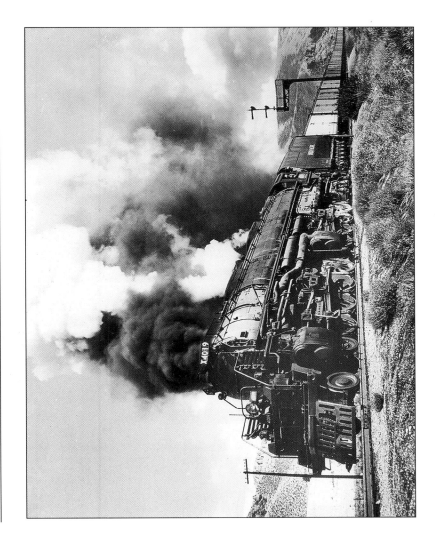

OPPOSITE

ABOVE: The eastbound Grand Canyon Limited out of Los Angeles, headed by a 4-8-4 Santa Fe 3765-class locomotive, runs round a freight train in Cajon Pass, California, in the1940s.

BELOW: An ROD locomotive hauls a train-load of British troops on freight wagons towards the Western Front, 29 August 1917.

ABOVE: Union Pacific's articulated Big Boy-class 4-8-8-4, hauling a string of freight cars through Echo Canyon, Utah in the early 1950s. Lcomotives of this type were developed from the 1930s.

28

LEFT: *A Merry-go-round coal train at Didcot station, England.*

BELOW LEFT: *Norfolk & Western class Y6B articulated locomotive 2185 being assembled at the Roanoke yard, 21 May 1949.*

BELOW: *Burlington Northern coal train loading in the mid-1970s.*

OPPOSITE: *An American Big Boy, perhaps the definitive locomotive for heavy freight haulage.*

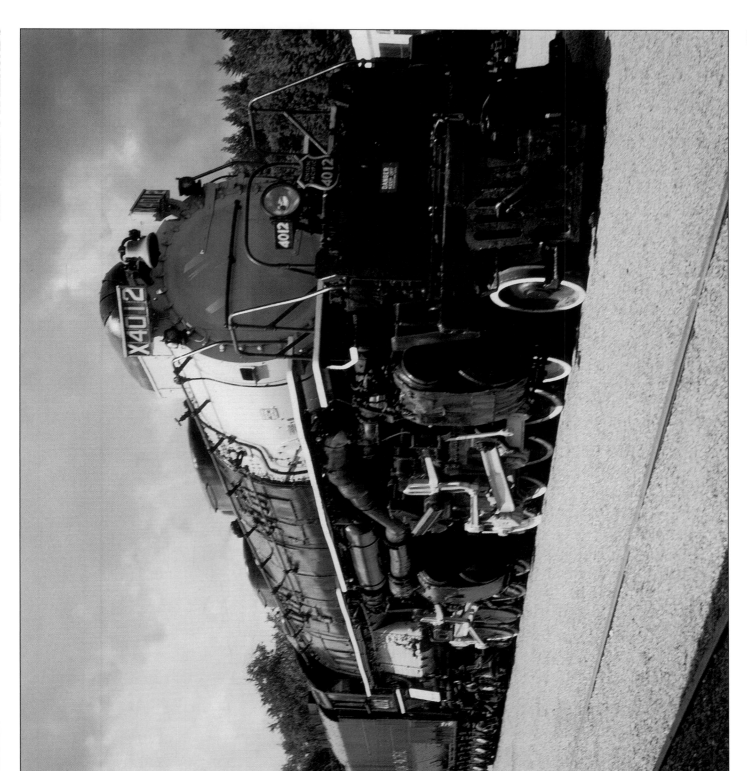

iron ore and other essential minerals) were wholly instrumental in the development of the U.S.A. as a major industrial nation. As the technology to do so became available, many of these little railroad lines were electrified, but most of the purely coal-mine railroads have faded from existence as other technologies have become available to extract the coal and lift it to the surface. Even so, coal is still a very important freight item for the main-line railroad operators.

China is another geographically vast country in which the availability of significant coal and mineral deposits has played a major part in the industrialization and general modernization of the country, especially in the years following the communist assumption of power in 1949. Thus the experience of the Chinese had mirrored that of the Americans, albeit a century or more later and in a country that was not almost empty but rather filled virtually to the limit with people. The railroads associated with the huge Chinese coal fields have for many years been the province mostly of tender locomotives from their earliest stages and then more recently by the 'SY' class of 2-8-2 standard locomotives built at Tangshan. The scale of the Chinese operation combines with the ability of the communist government to dictate that economic and political considerations should prevail over all else to generate a situation completely different from those that existed in the early days of British and European coal-field exploitation. As a result, the scale of the Chinese operation is larger on every level, and this

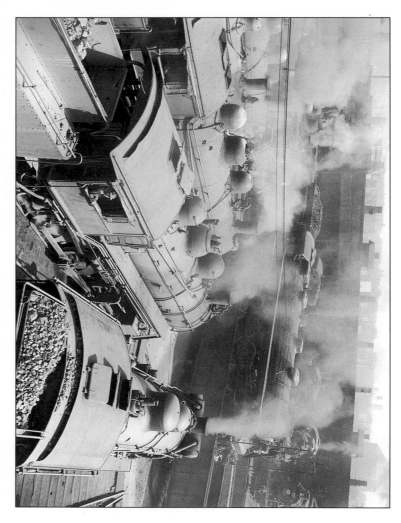

ABOVE: Locomotives of the Canadian National Railway were serviced and assigned to trains from 'roundhouses', like this one in Montreal.

Revolution, not only in being wholly necessary for the sparking of this movement and then its subsequent growth, but also in the vast volume and weight of the two commodities that must be transported. Thus there are many parallels between the railroad systems, together with their associated locomotives and rolling stock, involved in the coal and mineral ore exploitation industries. The first locomotive for use on a railroad transporting iron ore is thought to have been the unit that started work at Irthlingborough in Northamptonshire in 1867, but the British iron-ore industry is now dead, partially as a result of the high cost of transporting the ore between points in the U.K. but more as a consequence of the availability of superior imported ores, such as that from Sweden that typically contains 55 per cent iron rather than the 23 per cent iron that was the maximum contained in British ore.

Among the most interesting of the railways connected with the British iron-ore industry was that in and around the steel town of Corby in the English Midlands' county of Northamptonshire. Here the steel works operated their own railway that extended in a series of extensive branch lines reaching out into the country round the town to deliver a constant supply of iron ore from the various pits. In its heyday during the 1950s, as the U.K. was rebuilding its industrial base after World War II, the steel industry at Corby operated a large fleet of tank engines for its mines division and another large fleet for its steel works. This railroad system was not limited only to

Corby and its environs, moreover, for the Northamptonshire ironstone fields were extensive enough to be used to feed ore to other great steel-making areas, and as a result the Corby railroad system was closely interconnected with the main-line network so that iron-ore trains, sometimes as many as ten per day, could be hauled to other steel-making centres in Nottinghamshire and Yorkshire.

In continental Europe, one of the most fascinating iron-ore railroads using steam locomotives was the Erzberg, or 'iron mountain', railroad of Austria-Hungary. Inaugurated in 1891 and based on a standard-gauge railroad track, this line was used to transport iron ore from the mining site on the mountain (though large hill might be a more apt description) to the steel works at Donawitz, a distance of 121 miles (195km). One of the most interesting features of this railroad, which is still operational and has a ruling gradient of 1/14 over much of its length, is the use of both rack traction for the steeper gradients and adhesion traction for the flat and less steeply inclined sections of the route. The standard locomotive for the route was the type of 0-6-2T four-cylinder rack and traction engine built between 1890 and 1908 by Wiener Lokomotivfabrik, and this could haul a train of up to 110 tons. Similar arrangements were used in other European countries where iron-ore deposits were found at some distance, vertically as well as horizontally, from the industrial regions at which the ore was processed. Another notable iron-ore railroad was that inaugurated in Australia in 1932 to

provides no more fascinating a fact than that the Chinese can therefore operate genuinely larger main-line type locomotives in the coal exploitation industry rather than the genuinely small 0-6-0 and similar colliery locomotives that were typical of British and European practices. Another very striking contrast is that while the steam locomotive has long since disappeared from the British, European and U.S. coal-mining industries, where the smaller numbers of current types are of the diesel-powered variety, it is still very much alive in China and is likely to remain so until well into the 21st century.

As suggested above, railroads for the exploitation of coal and mineral ores are twins within the context of the Industrial

coincide with the establishment of an Australian steel works at Port Kembla in New South Wales. A railroad was driven up the steep mountainsides of the region to connect the rapidly-growing industrial area with Moss Vale junction with the main line. Some 43-miles (69-km) long, the line was in its time one of the world's lengthiest, purely industrial railroad lines.

With iron ore just as much as with coal, China has one of the most elaborate and extensive specialized railroad systems in the world. In this instance, the centre of this huge undertaking is the Anshan region of northern China, where there are huge deposits of iron ore as well as of coal. The quarries from which the iron ore is extracted are linked to the city and its industrial areas by a circular railroad over which trains move passengers as well as iron ore. In this fashion, the industrial areas of Anshan are fully supplied with both raw materials and a workforce. Oddly enough, this railroad is operated with electrical power, the locomotives being of design and manufacturing dates somewhat earlier than the equivalent dates for the steam locomotives still extensively used on China's main-line services. The Anshan complex comprises 12 control areas, including 15 main lines from which a host of branch lines diverge, and at any time there are over 100 locomotives in use.

While the railroad system employed to move iron ore to American steel-manufacturing centres is not in any way radically different from that of any other similar system in the industrialized world,

ABOVE: *Baltimore & Ohio Railroad coal train.*

LEFT: *A heavy iron-ore train on the Québec Cartier Mining Company Railway, Canada.*

ABOVE: *A double-headed steam train hauls mixed freight on the Jingpeng line. China has one of the most elaborate and specialized railroad systems in the world.*

LEFT: *Three Krauss-Maffei diesel-hydraulic power units haul a Denver & Rio Grande mixed freight train over the Rockies.*

OPPOSITE: *A Chinese coal train on the Nanking bridge. Coal and iron ore are hauled extensively by rail in China.*

the very size of many American steel mills means that they usually possess large railroad networks in and around their plants. The plant lines are often of the standard-gauge type, and this offers the very useful capability for the simple interchange of freight cars between the main line and the plant line. The locomotives used on the plant lines have in more recent times generally been of the diesel-powered type, but an odd exception up to 1980 was North Western Steel & Wire of Sterling, Illinois, which up to that date still operated steam locomotives. With the decline of the steel industry in the U.S.A. as a result of declining demand and the availability of cheaper imported steel, many mills have closed, thereby removing virtually all demand for these specialized railroads; yet in the late 1990s a few steel-mill railroad lines are still operational.

The close relationship between coal and iron ore in terms of railroad requirement is mirrored, with obvious changes, by the interrelationship between any industrialized nation's railroad network and sea ports, which still provide the essential interface between domestic and international transport of the vast majority of bulky and weighty imports and exports. For this reason many main-line tracks are continued right into the dock area, but there are also many ports in which there is a separate railroad system for the docks, thus providing a mobile 'bridge' between the land and the sea so that goods can be transferred between cargo vessels and main-line railroads. As with coal mine and ore

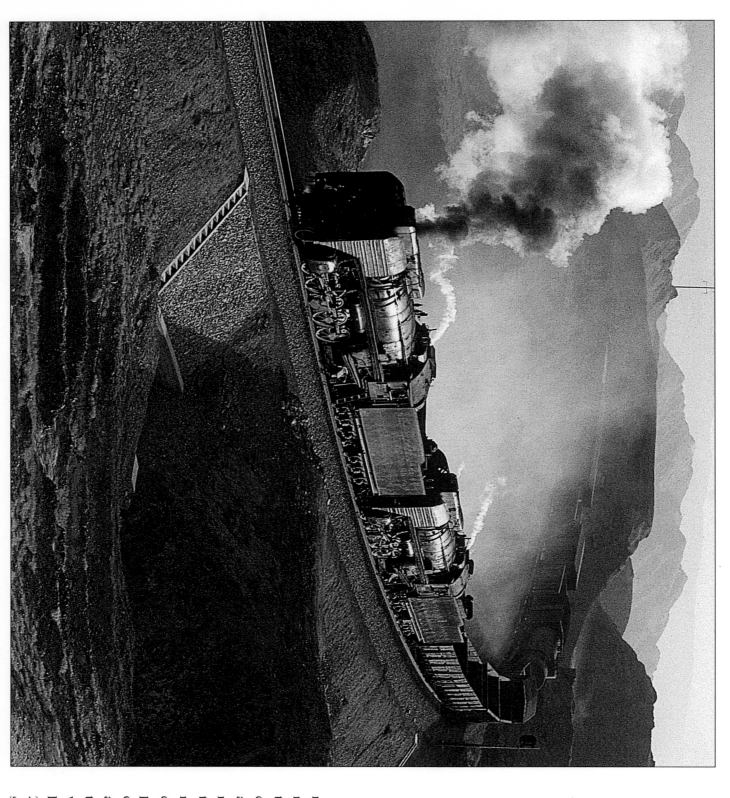

LEFT: Two Chinese QJ-class locomotives haul freight in the Gobi desert of inner Mongolia. 'QJ' stands for Qiang Jing or 'March Forward'.

OPPOSITE
ABOVE: Three J's thrash out of Banking station on the Chengde steelworks branch in China.

BELOW: Narrow-gauge iron-ore train in Koolanooka Hills, Western Australia.

railroad systems, the type of railroad needed for effective use in the confines typical of most ports involved small-radius curves and other restrictions on size, and as a result the typical port railroad system relies on small engines, most typically of the tank-locomotive type when such railroads were operated by steam-powered engines. Even so, the need for considerable power for the movement of heavy loads often required the juxtaposition of small and large engines, and a typical system of this type was that of the Bombay Port Trust, which had large 2-10-2 tank engines for hump-shunting and also somewhat smaller 2-6-0 tank engines for the movement of smaller loads.

should be noted that in the complex of the Brooklyn Eastern District steam-powered locomotives were still in comparatively large-scale service right into the 1960s, which was considerably later than the survival of similar locomotives in other large American ports.

Connected to the port conceptually and often physically, the shipbuilding yard has generally relied on the receipt of its basic raw materials, both steel sheet and in later years prefabricated sections, by railroad. The raw materials are then usually distributed within the yard by the shipbuilder's own railroad system. Typical of such a system, which is not as prevalent as it used to be as a result of the more extensive use of trucks and travelling cranes, was the Doxford shipyard at Sunderland in the north-east of England. This yard was revised during the early part of the 20th century with an internal railroad system amounting to 13 miles (21km) of track and based essentially on the use of steam-crane locomotives. The first of these, built by Hawthorn, Leslie of neighbouring Newcastle upon Tyne and providing a 9,000-lb (4082-kg) lift capability, was operating by 1904 and remained in service up to 1971, not because the locomotive was deemed obsolete for its purpose but rather for a number of unrelated factors such as shortages of spare parts and the introduction locally of a smokeless zone policy. The whole of the Doxford railroad system was then abandoned, roads being laid over the tracks and the crane-tank engine concept being abandoned in favour

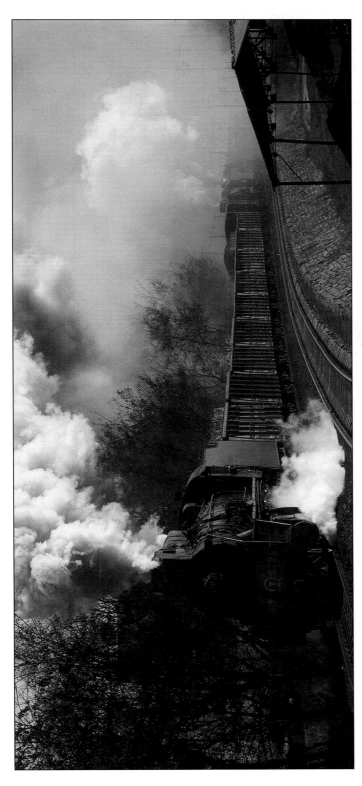

The larger sea ports of the U.S.A., typified by New York on the east coast and San Francisco on the west were and, to a more limited extent, still are characterized by complex networks of quayside railroad tracks and car-float operations. These lines were usually of the standard-gauge type for maximum interchangeability of traffic between the port network and the main-line system. Another notable feature of the port railroad networks was the fact that they included a high proportion of street running, resulting in the setting of the tracks in the roadway, the general use of small-radius curves and trim clearances, and the general use of light switch engines for motive power. These port railroad systems were among the first to be served by diesel-electric locomotives, although it

of the combination of fork-lift trucks and mobile road cranes.

The construction of large ships took place in only a comparatively small number of places in global terms, and the single most important area for shipbuilding in the later half of the 19th century and the first quarter of the 20th century was Clydeside in the Scottish city of Glasgow: it is estimated that during this period as many as four out of every five of the worlds' merchant ships were launched from Glaswegian yards, where the 'maid-of-all-work' locomotive was the Scottish 0-4-0 saddle-tank, or 'pug', engine. There were, of course, a number of other major shipbuilding centres in other parts of the world, especially in Europe and the U.S.A., and those which included a significant railroad system numbered among their total Belfast, Gdansk, Hamburg, Kiel, Malmö and Rostock.

Another type of railroad operation that has existed virtually from the beginning of rail transport has been that associated with logging or, more specifically, the extraction of the felled timber from logging areas. Under circumstances ideal for the railroad operator, of course, logging operations should take place near an existing railroad track, but life is never as conveniently arranged as that, so there has always to be a means of shifting the timber from the site of its felling to the nearest practical railroad. This originally meant the use of expedients such as the use of gravity to roll logs down mountainsides, or dragging them, or floating them down a nearby river. By the

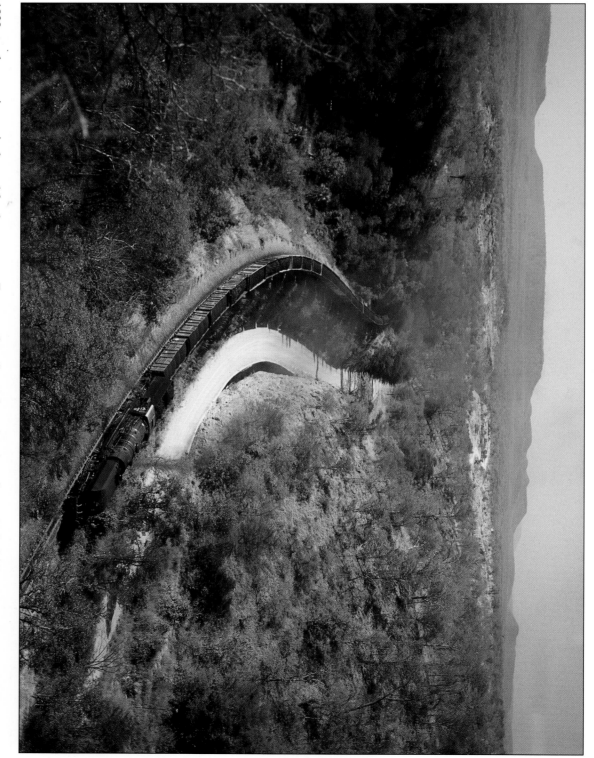

1920s trucks were increasingly used for the task of delivering felled timber to the railroad, but the increasing capability of trucks to carry very heavy loads and move across rough terrain has meant a considerable erosion of the railroad's responsibilities in this task.

For some time the north-west region of the U.S.A.'s and Canada's western seaboard on the Pacific Ocean, in the states of Oregon and Washington and the province of British Columbia respectively, has been one of the world's most important and technically advanced logging areas. Here

U.S. timber companies used logging railroads to deliver timber from the location being worked to the processing area where the saw mills were located, but as the area where trees were being felled altered on a steady basis, the railroads were generally built as lightly as possible with curves and

OPPOSITE: *In Africa, as in many countries of the world, specialized trains haul coal to stoke the fires of industry.*

THIS PAGE
FAR LEFT: *Heavy 'piggy-back' freight loads require powerful pulling power – here supplied by six power units.*

LEFT: *A Burlington Northern container train leaves the south Seattle yards.*

BELOW: *A Novatrans trailer, used either on train or truck, being loaded onto a ship.*

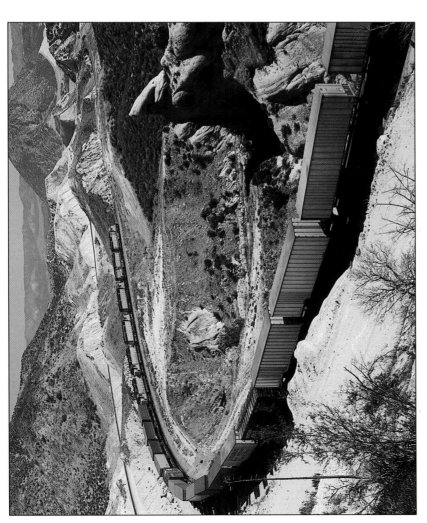

gradients that would not have been considered for more permanent railroads. During the period when steam was the driving force, specially designed geared locomotives were used for effective movement along these steep and winding routes. The type of locomotive most widely used for the task was the Shay, made by Lima, and using a row of vertical cylinders to drive a cranked shaft. Logging railroads made use of a variety of specialized cars to move raw timber, this role-specific equipment including free-wheel sets without frames that could be attached to large logs for movement over the rails.

It is worth noting that major logging railroads were once located in the northern part of the New England states, the central part of the Appalachian region including the states of Kentucky, Pennsylvania and West Virginia, the Sierra mountain region of the state of California, and the Cascade region of the Pacific North-West. Only a very small number of these specialized railroads still remain in operation.

As noted above, the particular nature of logging railroads led to the development of a number of special equipment items, and these included articulated locomotives, of which certainly the most celebrated was the

Shay. Pioneered in 1880 after development by Ephraim Shay, a Michigan logging engineer, the concept of the Shay locomotive was adopted by the Lima locomotive manufacturing company of Ohio. The Shay was built largely for the domestic American market, and most of the locomotives were of the standard-gauge type although modest numbers were also completed in a narrow-gauge format for export markets in Australia, eastern Asia and South America. Typical of the operators of Shay locomotives in eastern Asia was the Insular Lumber Company on Negros Island in the Philippines, which had a railroad of 3ft 6in (1.067m) gauge to deliver teak logs from the island's mountainous interior to the saw mills located near the coast: the logging trains halted on a ledge and a mechanical system then pushed sideways off the cars to fall a long distance into an artificial lake beside the saw mills.

On the other side of the world, not insignificant numbers of Feldbahn (field railway) locomotives built for the German

army in World War I ended their days in the logging role that was, after all, little different in its overall nature from the military railway for which the locomotives had been manufactured. The last Feldbahn locomotives were used at Czarna Bialystoka, a 75-mile (120-km) forestry system close to Bialystok in Poland on the main line from Warsaw to St. Petersburg (then Leningrad), and these steam locomotives were replaced by diesel locomotives built in Karl Marx Stadt in what was then East Germany but which has returned to its original name of Chemnitz in a unified Germany.

As with so many other features of its accelerated emergence into the 20th century from the time of the communists' 1949 victory in the civil war, China was a comparatively late entrant into the field of logging operations that are, in common with many other elements of the Chinese push towards modern industrialization and economic development, centred in the northern part of the country. Large numbers of 2ft 6in (0.76m) gauge railroads are here

employed on the movement of semi-trimmed logs from the felling sites to main-line junctions for further transport through Manchuria to all other parts of China.

The production of sugar is a major industry in several parts of the world, and the growth in the number and/or extent of sugar plantations to satisfy the cravings of an increasingly sweet-toothed world coincided with the industrialization that made sugar refining more efficient and also more exploitable as the finished product could then be moved in bulk by railroad to a port for export. As with many other industries, there also developed the concept of using narrow-gauge railroads within the manufacturing (in this instance growing and refining) site to expedite the whole process. This was especially important for sugar cane, which is grown in hot regions and can lose much of its important moisture (and with it much of the sugar) if there is any delay between cutting and processing. As a result, the spread of sugar-plantation railroads was rapid, and this type of operation was soon to be found in

ABOVE FAR LEFT: A mixed train of privately-owned and Freightliner containers.

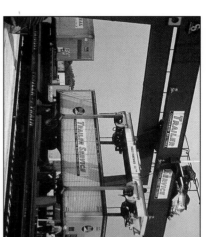

SECOND LEFT: Loading piggy-back trailers onto Baltimore & Ohio flatcars.

THIRD LEFT: Containers enable goods to be transferred easily from rail to ship and road.

ABOVE: Loading logs onto the narrow-gauge Chai He logging railway, China.

OPPOSITE

ABOVE: Transporting molten metal from the Krupp blast furnaces to a steel plant in a special torpedo wagon.

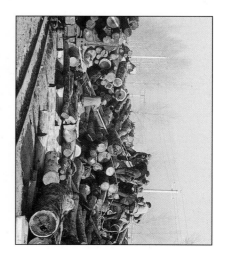

BELOW: Automatic track-lifting and ballast-tamping machine on a Baltimore & Ohio line keeps the wheels rolling.

Australia, Brazil, Cuba, Fiji, India, Java, Mauritius and the Philippines.

Java is typical of the regions economically reliant, at least in part, on the production of sugar. This Indonesian (originally Dutch) island in south-east Asia has more than 50 sugar refineries, many of them interconnected by a railroad system that is without doubt one of the most fascinating steam networks of the present day. The 2ft 3.5in (0.70m) gauge predominates, but some factories have railroads of 1ft 11.5in (0.60m) gauge, and the basic concept is based on a spoke-like arrangement of some 50 miles (80km) of track radiating from the refinery. One of the most attractive features of this apparently anachronistic system of steam railroads, which is also typical of Indian and Filipino operations, is its self-sufficiency in terms of fuel, for the locomotives use bagasse, which is compacted and baled sugar-cane fibres

created as a by-product of the sugar-refining process, as their essentially free fuel. The fuel provides little, though adequate, thermal energy for its volume, and as a result sugar-plantation railroads generally use tender-tank engines.

Sugar is not solely a product of sugar-cane plantations in the tropics, for a chemically identical sugar is produced from the sugar beet that is extensively grown in more temperate regions of the world. The

refining of sugar from pulped beet was introduced as early as 1747, and the system was established on a commercial basis during 1801 in the German state of Silesia. Since that time the production of sugar from beet has become an important industry in countries seeing the commercial advantage of not having to import their sugar, these including most northern

European nations as well as the U.S.A., where the primary beet-growing states are those of California and Oregon, where the beets are moved to large processing mills by railroad in specially designed cars. As in the tropical regions that have their own railroad systems, major sugar-beet centres in temperate climes often have an internal railroad system.

Despite the emergence of alternative technologies, much of the world's electricity is still produced with the aid of steam, even if the steam that powers the electricity-generating turbine equipment is now generated by nuclear reactors, gas and other heat sources rather than coal. But for nearly 100 years it was the coal-fired power station that was the core of any modern

country's electricity generating system, and this demanded the delivery to the power stations of very large quantities of coal, a task that could be achieved only by railroad. Thus the steam locomotive was a vital link in the chain between the coal mine and the power station, and until the 1950s and the large-scale introduction of diesel-powered equipment was the only effective means to

ABOVE: Logs being loaded onto a train of the Finnish state railway. Timber has been transported by rail almost since the beginning of the railroads.

LEFT: A log train being hauled by an 0-8-0 heading towards Chai He, China.

OPPOSITE: A Baldwin 2-8-0 locomotive of 1914 is still in active service and is here passing through La Vega in Cuba with a loaded cane train.

derived from coal at special gasworks established in towns providing a ready market for the gas. The production of gas was therefore reliant on the steady delivery of large quantities of coal, a fact which could be assured only by the railroad network. The production of gas from coal became viable in the 1830s, at much the same time that the railroad concept was beginning to spread its wings, and the development of the two went very much hand-in-hand, with the gas works often located close to the railroad station. The vital nature of the railroad is suggested by the fact that it was needed not only to bring in the coal, but also to take away by-products such as coke and coal tar, the latter of increasing importance to the chemical and pharmaceutical industries that grew so important from the middle of the century.

Probably the largest complex of its time anywhere in the world was the gas works at Beckton in the eastern part of London, the British capital. Here there were some 90miles (145km) of track, whose traffic was hauled by a class of small 0-4-0 side-tank locomotives designed and built specifically for this task by Neilson Reid of Glasgow. These locomotives ran in everyday service from the early 1880s until their retirement in the mid-1960s.

So far, most of the freight-hauling roles considered above have been of the heavy industrial type, even though logging and sugar obviously do not fall directly into this category; but it should not be forgotten that the railroad also found ready niches outside the industrial scene, most notably for the

deliver coal in the required quantities. In basic terms, high-quality coal (otherwise known as 'steam' coal) was generally delivered by main-line railroad to the railhead and reception yard as close to the power station as possible, and then shifted from this to the power stations in cars hauled by side- and saddle-tank locomotives, generally of the 0-4-0 and

0-6-0 types. The best possible solution was, of course, the location of a power station as close as possible to the coal mine, but this was generally possible only in countries that came late to industrialization. Typical of these was India, which was able to create in the state of Madhya Pradesh a huge electricity generating complex at Korba, only 10 miles (16km)

from the source of its coal at Manikpur.

Another basic source of power for domestic and industrial purposes is flammable gas, and before the development of the natural gas industry, which relies on vast networks of pipelines and special ships to move adequate quantities of this fuel from the regions in which it is extracted from oil or other natural deposits, this was

41

movement of large loads of rural commodities. Some of the more interesting of these that have become associated with railroad transport include fibres such as cotton and jute (and by extension wool in countries such as Australia), palm oil, potatoes, peanuts or ground nuts, grains, and even peat.

As far as cotton is concerned, the world's most extensive railroad operation is that of the Gezira Project in Sudan. This radiates from Wad el Shatie, and comprises very many miles of 1ft 11.5in (0.60m) gauge track over which the cotton-carrying cars are hauled by Hunslet 0-8-0 diesel locomotives. Railways for carrying jute

have been built, most notably in India and Bangladesh. As in munitions plants and paper mills, the category of locomotive chosen for this task, at least within the processing works, is of the fireless steam type which draws its working supply of steam from a static source to avoid the danger, almost inevitable with a conventional steam locomotive, that sparks from the firebox or smokestack could set fire to the load in the towed cars or in the fields beside the track.

On the Indonesian island of Sumatra, one of the main industries is the extraction of palm oil, a commodity that is used in the manufacture of soap and margarine.

Enormous quantities of the fruit have to be delivered from the plantations to the mills, a task achieved by the use of steam locomotives on several narrow-gauge railroad systems radiating from the factories into the plantations and operated by 0-4-4-0T Mallet-type locomotives manufactured in the Netherlands, while the Indonesian archipelago was still the Dutch East Indies, by Ducroo & Brauns. A natural waste product of the palm-oil process, namely the hard shell of the kernel, is burned as fuel in the locomotives, thereby reducing the direct operating costs of the system, and an advantage of this fuel by comparison with the bagasse used on sugar

plantations, is its high thermal value.

Reflecting the vast tonnage of foodstuffs delivered from the hinterland of Argentina to the nation's ports for export, as befitting the former position of this South American country as the 'larder of the world' and one of the world's leading economies, the potato railroads were once a part of the Buenos Aires & Great Southern Railway. These railroads comprised a large system of tracks, in 2ft 0in (0.61m) gauge, for the movement of trains, carrying loads as diverse as potatoes, wheat and beef, hauled initially by Hunslet 4-6-0 locomotives which had been rendered surplus to British army requirement in the

hauled by diesel locomotives to the plants at which it is milled and compressed into briquettes for use in domestic fires or as the power source for electricity generating stations, where it is blown into the furnaces in the same way as other pulverized fuels.

There are several types of agricultural railroad in North America. Perhaps the best known, and also probably the most important, are the railroads that service the grain elevators that are so characteristic of the mid-western regions of the U.S.A. Often of very large size, these grain elevators are used for the storage of longer-life harvest products, usually wheat and corn, and most of the more substantial

aftermath of World War I, but were later supplanted by Simplex petrol and diesel locomotives.

One of the most remarkable and extensive industrial railway operations in the world operates in the southern part of Ireland. The island lacks an indigenous supply of coal, but peat was found to be a cheap and efficient alternative as a primary fuel. As well as a fuel for domestic hearths, the peat can also be used in a number of industrial applications including service as a fuel for power stations. After the peat has been drained and cut, it is piled beside the 3ft (0.918m) gauge railroad lines laid across the bogs, from which the cut turves are

complexes are accessed by railroads operated by industrial switch engines, which shunt the main-line freight cars as they are loaded from the elevators.

In large parts of the world the development of the railroads and the discovery of new large-scale sources of important minerals coincided from the middle of the 19th century, and in many respects it is particular way without the other. One of the world's largest suppliers of gold, South Africa saw the coincident development of its railroad network and its gold-mining industry, the first reliant on the wealth brought in by the latter for its large-scale development, and the latter needing the former for the delivery of heavy equipment and the

movement of large quantities of the ore from which the pure gold was then smelted. Among South Africa's most significant gold mines was City Deep in the extraordinarily rich gold reef region around Johannesburg, and this operation was perhaps typical of its period in its completion with its railroad system that operated right through the day and night with the aid of six 4-8-4T locomotives manufactured by the North British Locomotive Company. This system allowed for the gold ore to be transported from the head of the two primary mineshafts to the mill, after which the crumbled ore was again moved by railroad to the Jupiter Station junction with the main line, from which the ore proceeded to the smelting facility. At least two other South African gold-mining operations had their

own railroad systems, in each case with the same type of North British 0-8-0T tank engines.

South Africa has and still does generate a large measure of its wealth from the country's extensive diamond deposits, and another rich source of diamonds was the neighbouring country of South-West Africa, which was originally a colony of Germany, which was initially responsible for the discovery and exploitation of the country's diamond wealth. The South-West Africa (now Namibia) diamond industry came into existence during the 1890s, and the modest railroads associated with the industry were remarkable in their use of first-generation electric locomotives, most of these being 0-4-0 and Bo-Bo types built in Germany by Siemens. The trains hauled by these

locomotives were used for the disposal of the rock and other waste materials from the diamond mines, whose management was assumed by the De Beers company after South African forces had taken South-West Africa from the Germans in World War I.

Farther to the north, but still on the western side of southern Africa, lies Angola that was a Portuguese colony but is now independent. In this country lies the Benguela railroad, which extends some 838 miles (1348km) between the port of Lobito and Luau on the border with the Congo, via Benguela itself. This railroad was created in the period between 1904 and 1929 as what was and still is the single most important outlet for the precious minerals mined in Central Africa. Until the Angolan Civil War in 1975, the Caminho Ferro de Benguela

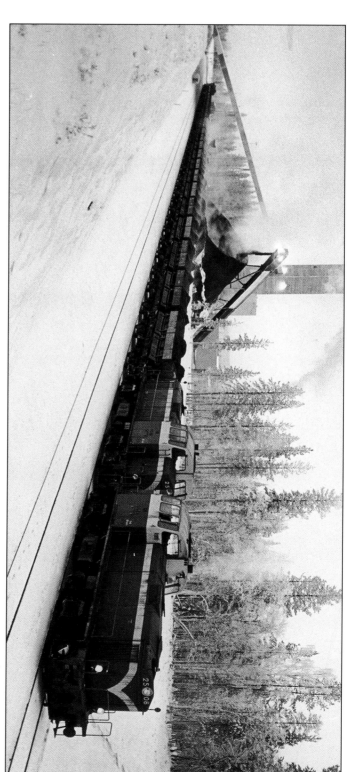

ABOVE: Dv 12- (formerly Sv 12-) class diesel-hydraulic locomotives haul a coal train past a loading point on the Finnish state railway.

was one of the most efficient railroads in Africa, and was owned by Tanganyika Concessions, a subsidiary of the Belgian firm of Union Minier. Angola is a troubled country still, and the reconstruction of the Benguela railroad is a prerequisite of a revived national economy.

A mineral that came to rival iron in the economy of the 20th century was aluminium, the metal extracted from bauxite ore of the type mined in countries such as Jamaica. The bauxite is found in the interior of the island, and both American and British financial resources were used to create the railroad by means of which the ore could be shifted from the mines to a junction with the Jamaica National Railway network for onward movement to the coast for export. The Jamaican railroad system was closed down in the middle of the 1980s, and the bauxite system is now the sole railroad operation in Jamaica. In the later part of the 1960s the original generation of steam locomotives was replaced by a more modern generation of American-built diesel-powered Bo-Bo and Co-Co locomotives. Large quantities of bauxite are also mined in India, where the major operation is that near Renukut. The aluminium smelting plant in this city is served by its own railroad system of 5ft 6in (1.683m) gauge, the primary task for this railroad being the delivery not of bauxite but of the very substantial amount of coal needed for the smelting operation. The most important of the locomotives used in this task are ex-main-line banking locomotives, whose great power makes them very

effective in the slow but steady delivery of massive loads of coal. Another country that is a major exporter of bauxite is Ghana on the west coast of Africa, and here narrow-gauge industrial railroads are used for the delivery of ore from the inland mining regions to junctions with the country's main-line network for onward transmission to the coast.

Another area of the world blessed, if that is the right word, with very important deposits of strategically important and therefore valuable minerals is the island of Tasmania off the south-eastern corner of the Australian continental land mass. Despite its comparatively small size, the island had been revealed to possess huge ore deposits from which tin, lead, silver, gold, copper and iron can be extracted. The terrain of this mountainous and highly forested island is too difficult for the cost-effective construction of major roads, so movement to and from the mineral deposits was generally achieved by tramways or railways. One of the earliest tramways, worked by horse power, was that built at the Mount Bischoff tin mine in 1878, but this was soon converted to a 3ft 6in (1.071m) gauge railroad with steam locomotives. The Mount Lyell operation constructed a 21-mile (34-km) switchback railroad line connecting its copper mine with the coast. Much of the railroad was cut through heavy forest, but it also included two 4.5-mile (7-km) long sections with gradients of 1/16 and 1/20, where the Abt rack and pinion system had to be used by the 0-4-2T locomotives, of which the first was

delivered for service from 1896.

Another important but massive commodity requiring movement in large quantities, mainly for use in the building industry, is stone in its many forms, ranging in size from the upper limit represented by large boulders to the smallest and most compact loads in the forms of gravel and sand. It is worth noting that some of the earliest railroad lines constructed in North America were intended for the movement of stone, typical of this being the opening, in 1826, of the 3-mile (4.8-km) Granite Railway at Quincy, Massachusetts for the animal-drawn transport of stone to the site of the Bunker Hill monument. The Chester & Becket operation, also in Massachusetts, hauled stone from quarries to Chester, where there were stone-cutting facilities and a connection with the main line. Other quarry lines were isolated from all other rail connections, and were used to move stones solely within the quarry facilities.

Interesting as they were, the stone railroads of New England, and indeed of many other parts of the U.S.A. as they were opened up for development, were relatively insignificant in relation to the Dutch (now Indonesian) railroad at Gunung Kataren on the island of Sumatra. This 1ft 3.75in (0.40m) gauge line was built to transport smooth, flat stones manually extracted from the bed of a fast river. From the river, the stones were hauled up to a primitive crusher located beside the state railroad's main line. Part of this line, employed for the generation of crushed stone for use as ballast, was an incline up which the wagons

had to be hauled individually by cable.

Even within the compass of a small and very crowded island nation such as England, there was ample scope for the development and extensive use of small company railroads, not only of the types mentioned above in connection with heavy industries such as coal mining, but also of more immediately consumer-oriented industries. Of these latter, those which could make most extensive use of company railway systems were the giants of the drink and food industries.

The most notable example of a railway owned and operated by a brewer was that of Bass, which operated a system involving private locomotives travelling over a 16-mile (25.5-km) track network connected with the main line at Burton-on-Trent. Of these 16 miles (25.5km), some 8 miles (13km) were located at Shobnall where there were maltings, a cask-washing plant, experimental bottling stores and beer-loading stations as well as sidings with the capacity for 400 wagons. Another 5 miles (8km) of track were used by the connections and sidings between the three main breweries, and the final 3 miles (5km) comprised the Dixie Exchange Sidings and Stores. The system was launched in 1862 and the expansion of the brewery was matched by that of its company railway: the existence of the railway in the middle of Burton-on-Trent meant that there were many crossings of public roads, and for reasons of safety Bass had to build signal boxes at the crossings. Such was the growth of Bass in the later part of the 19th century

46

and the early part of the 20th that by the 1920s the company's railway was undertaking the daily movement of more than 1,000 wagons, about one-third of them empty units returning from the main line and the other two-thirds involved in the transport within the brewery of materials such as malt, barley and coal.

Another brewing company with its own railway was Guinness, which had an extensive system in both 5ft 3in (1.596m) and 1ft 10in (0.56m) gauges at its Dublin brewery. This system, operated in parallel with barges on the River Liffey and the Irish main-line railway system, was the starting point for the delivery of Guinness stout to points all over Ireland and also for export trade.

Another type of British company railway was the 2-mile (3.2-km) system associated with the Port Sunlight refinery and commissioned during 1910 to link the refinery and margarine works with Bromborough Dock and the main-line station at Port Sunlight. In 1913 the operator bought from the North London Railway nine passenger coaches, and these were employed in the transport of workers to and from the main-line station. The Port Sunlight operation used 0-6-0T locomotives built especially for it by Andrew Barclay of Kilmarnock in Scotland. In the early part of the 20th century Cadbury, another economically shrewd but also philanthropic company, built a wide-ranging railway to serve its expanding chocolate factory at Bournville, near Birmingham. The railway was employed to bring in raw materials such as cocoa beans and the coal required to power the chocolate-making process, and

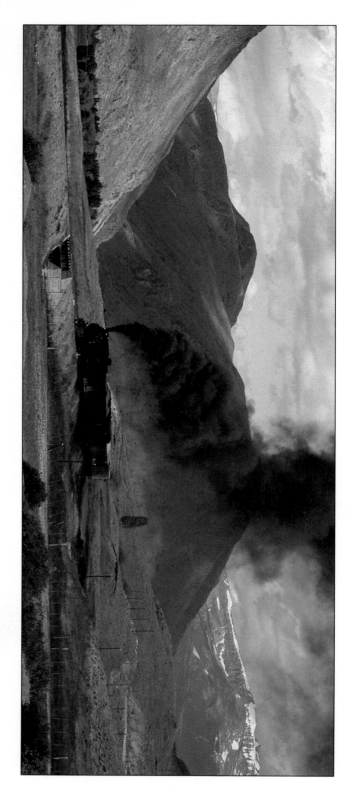

An Argentine narrow-gauge steam locomotive hauls a mixed load. In South America, the introduction of diesel power was sometimes limited because of the cost of imported diesel fuel relative to locally-mined coal.

also to delivery the finished products to the local main-line station for onward transport to all parts of the U.K. and indeed to very many other parts of the word.

As has been noted above, some of these small company railroads made use of diesel-powered locomotives, which in the first part of the 20th century had started the process of replacing the steam locomotive as the most important prime mover for heavy freight railroad services. In fact the first appearance of a diesel-engined locomotive as a main-line unit in North America took place in 1928, when the type entered service with the Rock Island Railroad. From this time onward, the position, once apparently unassailable, of the large steam locomotive for the hauling of heavy freight trains was first eroded and then over a period of some 40 years

ultimately destroyed by the diesel-engined locomotive. The diesel-engined locomotive was first adopted in significant numbers for main-line service during the mid- to late 1930s, when General Motors and General Electric, both giants of the American industrial scene, started to market and mass-produce suitable power units. The operators of main-line service in the U.S.A. were at first dubious about the viability of the new type of powerplant, but by the middle of World War II most of the companies had come round to the position in which they saw the diesel engine as the future of power for railroad purposes.

By the mid-1950s the diesel had become effectively paramount in North America, and as a result many classes of steam locomotive, many of them with only a few years of service under their belts,

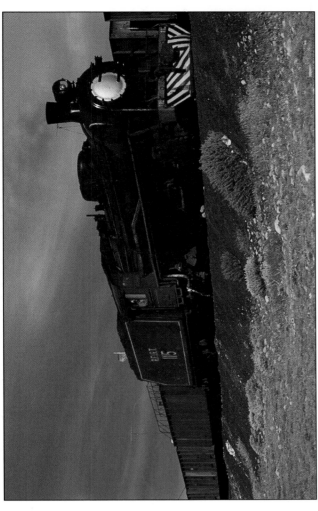

ABOVE LEFT: A South American 2-10-2 locomotive steams past another freight train at Rio Gallegos.

ABOVE: Another 2-10-2 South American locomotive. Many South American countries, lacking an indigenous manufacturing industry, relied on imports, particularly from America.

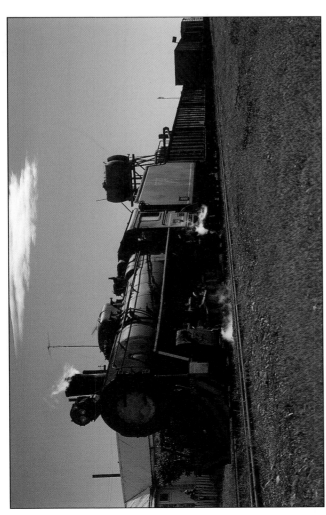

were withdrawn from service and scrapped. They were replaced by the units of the new 'E' and 'F' classes of standard locomotives, the former intended for express passenger work and the latter for mixed-traffic operations. For switching purposes and trip working the manufacturers produced a whole series of Bo-Bo and Co-Co single-cab hood types. With such motive power on the market, sold at reasonable terms and offering the attractions of reduced manning requirements, easier bunkering, greater fuel efficiency and reduced running costs, most railroads found it very attractive to 'dieselize' as soon and as rapidly as possible. The American manufacturers, which had attained a pre-eminent position as a result of their larger uninterrupted and therefore massive production of heavy transport equipment in World War II, were

also in the prime position to market their wares on the world stage, securing major success in Africa, Asia, Australia, New Zealand and South America. Some European countries, such as Spain and Portugal, also bought diesel locomotives from the U.S.A.

Diesel engines did not have matters all their own way, it should be noted, but they did come to predominate. An alternative to the diesel engine was the gas turbine of the type that had begun to mature for aircraft use in World War II and was extensively and rapidly refined after the war, and in the mid-1960s the Union Pacific Railroad decided to try an experiment with gas turbine traction. This was successfully achieved with a fleet of gas turbine units that were used primarily for heavy freight work on the Union Pacific Railroad's main

lines, and remained in operation until the late 1970s.

Diesel locomotives first appeared on the main-line services of the U.K. in the mid-1930s, when the Great Western Railway introduced streamlined diesel-powered railcars and parcel vans. Together with some later additions built in the 1940s, these remained in service up to the early 1960s. At the same time, the London, Midland & Scottish Railway also ordered diesel locomotives. At first these were just shunting locomotives, but later the railway constructed a three-car diesel multiple unit and, in 1947, ordered two diesel-powered main-line locomotives. In the same year the Southern Railway ordered three main-line diesel locomotives, but these were delivered only after the formation of the nationalized British Railways in 1948. These three

ABOVE LEFT: An early Canadian Northern Railway freight train passing a typical western grain elevator, circa 1915.

ABOVE: Baltimore & Ohio Railroad workshops at Piedmont, West Virginia at the foot of the 'Seventeen-Mile' grade from Piedmont to Altamont, Maryland, circa 1875.

FAR LEFT: Excavating for a 'Y' on the Orange & Alexandria Railroad. Brigadier-General Hermann Haupt, Chief of the U.S. Military Railroads, is standing on the bank supervising the work, the locomotive General Haupt heading the work train. From the early days, railways have carried men and materiel to battle.

LEFT: Track maintenance is crucial for safety.

and manufacture, but nonetheless based strongly on the technology of the American locomotives. The Soviet engines were not as good as their U.S. counterparts, however, and it was not until the 1980s, when other elements of outside technology were more readily tapped, that the Soviets were at last able to make significant strides and start the introduction of modern, efficient designs.

The development of diesel traction in Germany began during 1932 with the introduction of the famous and nicely streamlined *Flying Hamburger* three-car diesel units, which later led to the construction of several experimental main-line locomotives, both before and during the first part of World War II. The result of this process was the introduction, in the period after the end of World War II, of a fleet of modern locomotives of the diesel-hydraulic and diesel-electric types, and these supplanted steam locomotives for all main-line purposes from the late 1950s.

The Soviet state railway benefited greatly from the delivery of Lend-Lease equipment, mainly from the U.S.A. and including numbers of steam locomotives, in the course of World War II. In the period immediately after the war's end and before the dropping of the 'iron curtain', substantial numbers of diesel locomotives were also shipped to the U.S.S.R. from the U.S.A. Experience with these units persuaded the Soviet state railway organization in the 1950s that the time was ripe for these American units to be supplemented and then supplanted by diesel-engined locomotives of Soviet design

While the appearance of the diesel-engined locomotive was not greeted with the same level of approval as had generally been the case when the steam-powered locomotive made its initial appearance, this was probably the result of a certain blasé element in the perception of a public that had grown up with the railroad as part of its earliest memories, but also in part because early diesel-engined locomotives were both technically crude and, as a result of their limited power, poor in performance. The basic concept of the internal combustion engine had been established as early as 1794, but it was not until 1883 that Daimler patented the high-speed petrol engine, closely followed by the appearance of Rudolf Diesel's 'oil engine' in 1892. Two years later, the first locomotive to use this new form of power was built by Priestman

locomotives were the precursors of the '40' class of main-line locomotives used extensively during the 1960s. As a result of the technical success of these and other early experimental diesel-powered locomotives, British Railways was led to formulate the 1955 modernization plan that led, somewhat prematurely, to the elimination of steam locomotives from British main-line routes by 1968.

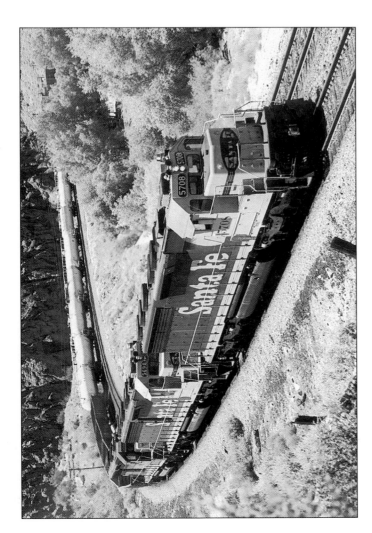

ABOVE: *Santa Fe's diesel locomotive No. 5708 carrying eastbound freight through Crozier Canyon in Arizona.*

RIGHT: *The famous Union Pacific Centennial-class locomotive hauls its load of piggy-back containers. The commissioning of this class was how Union Pacific chose to celebrate its 100 years of railway operation.*

Brothers of Hull: this was a 12-hp (8.9-kW) dockyard shunter with a diesel engine and mechanical transmission. In 1896, another diesel-engined locomotive was constructed for the Woolwich Arsenal in London: manufactured by Hornsby & Son of Grantham, this 9-hp (6.7-kW) single-cylinder machine was somewhat underpowered, but it was generally successful and its quickly proved capabilities were enough to persuade the War Office to order a further four.

The year 1912 was the time for the next breakthrough for the diesel-engined locomotive, for it was in this year that there appeared the world's first diesel-powered railcar. Built by the Sodermanland Midland Railway of Sweden, the railcar was an adapted coach, fitted with a diesel engine and generator. Further examples were made for other Swedish railways by Allmanna Svenska Aktiebolaget.

The ghastly years of World War I restricted the development of diesel motive power in the short term, so it was not until the 1920s that significant progress was once more achieved. It is worth noting, though, that petrol-engined railcars had been produced in the U.S.A. during this period when, in 1917, the General Electric Company built a railcar with electric transmission for the Delaware & Hudson Railroad. Moderately large numbers of similar petrol-engined railcars were soon operational on several railroad lines in the more rural regions of the U.S.A. The first really successful diesel-engined locomotive

was a 300hp (224kW) shunter constructed in 1924 by Alco, General Electric and Ingersoll Rand for the Jersey Central Lines, and some 26 basically similar locomotives were made in the next two years for various railways and industrial companies.

It was during the 1930s that the diesel-engined locomotive finally began to emerge as a major force in the American railroad system. Significant improvements in the technology of diesel engines, including a major boost in locomotive power/weight ratios through a reduction in weight and an increase in power, at last started to make diesel-engined locomotives an attractive commercial proposition to main-line railroads. Much of this new technology was used in the streamlined express trains such as the Burlington Railroad's *Pioneer Zephyr* that was introduced in 1934. The Union Pacific Railroad inaugurated its own streamlined diesel locomotives to service in the same year, and a measure of the importance of the new 1,200-hp (895-kW) locomotives was the fact that they allowed an 18-hour reduction of the scheduled time for the 2,270-mile (3653-km) journey between Chicago, Illinois and Portland, Oregon from October 1934.

The success of the diesel-powered locomotive in the U.S.A. can be seen as the single factor that was most important in opening the floodgates for this type of traction in other parts of the world, where diesel-engined streamlined locomotives began to appear in ever larger numbers to haul prestige express trains: the celebrated

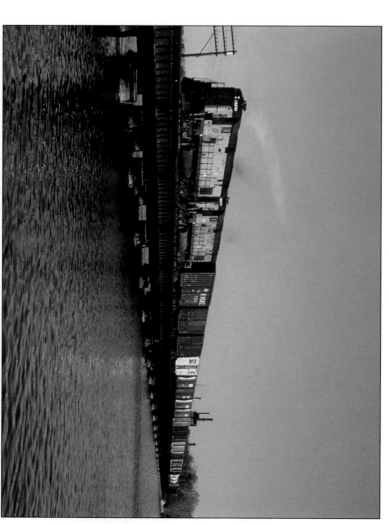

ABOVE: *Chicago & North Western-type C 624 locomotive, No. 6707 heads a mixed freight in Wisconsin.*

OPPOSITE
ABOVE LEFT: *Denver & Rio Grande diesel-hydraulic locomotive No. 4003. Built by Krauss-Maffei in Germany, these locomotives caused a stir when first introduced because American railroads had not imported locomotives since their earliest days.*

ABOVE RIGHT: *A Chicago & North Western RS-32 locomotive No. 4249-3, hauling scrap at Green Bay, Wisconsin.*

BELOW LEFT: *A British Petroleum company train consisting of 100-ton bogie tankers hauled by a diesel-electric British Rail locomotive.*

BELOW RIGHT: *A switcher at Joliet, Illinois with covered hoppers loaded with phosphate.*

Flying Hamburger, built for the Deutsche Reichsbahn, was a glamorous propaganda tool for Nazi Germany, and there were similar streamlined units used on Austrian and French railways well before the outbreak of World War II in 1939.

However, this situation did not prevail in the U.K., where the 'big four' railway companies were still unconvinced of the merits of diesel power for the hauling of high-speed, main-line services and therefore restricted themselves to experiments with less powerful railcars on secondary or branch lines. In 1934 the Great Western Railway introduced a new diesel-engined railcar, developed in conjunction with the bus manufacturer AEC. This was sufficiently successful for the company to order a further 17 such engines before building another 20 units of its own design at Swindon.

As noted above, it was in the U.S.A. that there appeared the main impetus for the replacement of the steam locomotive with the diesel locomotive. General Motors began this process in 1937 with the construction of its first 'E1'-class 1,800-hp (1342-kW) passenger locomotive, which was doubly significant as it was also the first standardized design. Customers could choose single-cab or cabless power units, setting a trend in U.S. railroading as operators could now 'mix and match' power units. Less than two years later the 'E6'-class diesel locomotive, a more powerful 2,000-hp (1491-kW) version of the E1, was manufactured and this was followed in 1939 by the 'FT' class, which

OPPOSITE

ABOVE: Heavy-duty freight sometimes required the support of 'helper' locomotives, particularly up steep inclines.

BELOW: The celebrated Flying Hamburger, the glamorous German streamlined diesel express of the 1930s. The process of adoption of diesel power in the U.S.A. spread to Europe in a more diffuse, less dramatic way.

RIGHT: The legendary Union Pacific Big Boy-class 4-8-8-4 locomotive, in its day the most powerful locomotive in the world.

was a freight-hauling version of the E6-class locomotive.

In the next 10 years the speed with which dieselization overtook the steam locomotive in the U.S.A. was remarkable. The rate of this process is indicated by the fact that while there were a mere 314 diesel-engined locomotives on American railroads during 1938, the total had increased to nearly 12,000 by 1950. Looked at the other way round, the total of 40,000 or more steam-powered locomotives in service during 1939 had declined to only just over 15,000 such locomotives by 1950.

This development in the success and popularity of the diesel-engined locomotive was not merely an increase represented in terms of numbers or horse power, but also an improvement in the basic qualities of the diesel-powered locomotive. In the period after the end of World War II, for instance, the 'road switcher' or 'hood' type of locomotive made its appearance as a development of the basic locomotive with a full-width cab and the engine contained within a narrow hood, allowing the provision of an external walkway on each side. The locomotives of this type were certainly less attractive in visual terms than their predecessors, but also offered better fields of vision to the front and rapidly became a typical aspect of North American railroad operations. Evidence of this fact is provided by the delivery by General Motors' Electro-Motive Division of considerably more than 10,500 'GP' type of road switcher engines to American railroads between 1949 and 1975: the early 1,500-hp (1118-kW) 'GP7' class was superseded by ever more powerful variations, so that power ratings of 3,600hp (2684kW) were available in the 1960s.

In 1969 there made its appearance the world's largest and most powerful type of single-unit diesel locomotive. This 'Centennial' class was built for the Union Pacific Railroad by General Motors, and its class name celebrated the centenary of the

53

driving in of the gold-plated 'last spike' of the transcontinental railroad. Production totalled 47 locomotives, each with a 6,600-hp (4921-kW) engine. The Union Pacific Railroad was not typical of most North American railroad operators, most of which were content to operate with lower-powered locomotives that could be boosted by the addition of 'slave' units coupled to the main locomotive according to the weight of the load being moved.

By the 1960s, only two main manufacturers dominated the scene in the U.S.A., namely General Motors and General Electric, while the celebrated names of the previous generations, such as Alco, Baldwin, Fairbanks-Morse and Lima that had dominated the age of steam, had effectively disappeared.

In Europe the introduction of the diesel-engined locomotive was more diffuse and less dramatic than the equivalent process in the U.S.A. A number of countries opted to make their beginnings on the basis of American expertise, and therefore contracted with American companies such as General Motors to build and equip their railways with diesel-powered locomotives. This was the case in Sweden, although by the 1960s the state railroad system was operated by almost equal numbers of diesel-engined and electrically powered locomotives. General Motors also had considerable success in Denmark where, as recently as 1981, units of the 3,240-hp (2416-kW) 'ME' class were ordered for passenger and goods traffic. In Spain, locomotives from another American

company, Alco, were also purchased.

Elsewhere in Europe the situation was much more varied. In France and Italy the railroads produced their own diesel-powered locomotives. The most individualistic approach was that of West Germany. After World War II, German manufacturers and the Deutsche Bundesbahn placed their faith in the locomotive with diesel-hydraulic motive power as they believed that the combination of a high-speed engine and hydraulic transmission would result in locomotives that were both powerful and reliable. Krauss-Maffei built five prototype locomotives of this type in 1953, each of these prototypes being fitted with a pair of 1,100-hp (820-kW) Maybach engines. The trials of these prototypes were successful, so the Deutsche Bundesbahn ordered 100 examples of the generally similar 'V220' class, which was the inspiration for the 'D800'-class diesel-hydraulic locomotives manufactured for British Railways' Western Region at Swindon in 1960. However, the maintenance of this type of motive system proved to be expensive, so little use was made of its concept outside these two countries.

On the first day of 1948 the Labour government's plan for the nationalization of the British railway system was implemented and British Railways came into existence. Initially the new organization was not radical in its planning, so there was no large-scale move toward dieselization. However, this changed drastically with the publication of the 1955 modernization plan,

ABOVE: *An early locomotive on the Emmenthal-Burgdorf-Thun mountain railway. Not only did these locomotives head passenger trains, they also delivered freight and mail to isolated mountain communities.*

ABOVE RIGHT: *Steam engine on the rack-and-pinion Schafbergbahn, mid-1970s.*

RIGHT: *An electric engine hauling freight at the beginning of the 20th century.*

OPPOSITE
ABOVE: *Class 1189 Crocodile electric locomotive of the Austrian state railway, mid-1970s.*

BELOW: *Great Northern Railway early electric locomotives with a freight train.*

which called for the replacement, in as short a time as possible, of all British steam-powered locomotives with modern tractive equipment characterized by diesel or electric power. In other parts of Europe, in particular France and Germany, a much more strategic approach was taken, and as a result steam locomotives were retired over a number of years as they approached the ends of their useful lives: so while steam disappeared from British tracks by 1968, in Germany it was 1975 before it finally bowed out.

Despite its attempt to emulate the American railroads' rapid transition from steam to diesel power, the British did not want to use American technology and therefore turned to British companies for the design and manufacture of the new fleet

ABOVE: *A Baltimore & Ohio F-series all-purpose diesel-electric locomotive at east St. Louis, Illinois. The 'A' units had a driver's cab, the 'B' or 'Booster' units did not.*

LEFT: *The Baltimore & Ohio at Pittsburg, Pennsylvania. Unfortunately the glory days are over for this venerable locomotive.*

of diesel-engined locomotives. The results were highly mixed. In 1955, for example, the first of the 'Deltic' class was built by English Electric and later 22 more units were manufactured for service on the East Coast main line. Three years after the appearance of the Deltic, British Railways' Western Region opted for diesel-hydraulic rather than diesel-electric power, and the North British Locomotive Company was therefore contracted to produce the first diesel-hydraulic locomotive for British Railways. The resulting 'D600' class was unreliable and underpowered (and therefore soon retired), and was followed by the more powerful 'D800' class. In overall terms, the

(2982-kW) locomotive class. This latter was a double unit, and production exceeded 2,000 units in related passenger and freight versions.

In the rest of the world, especially Africa and South America, the ready acceptance of diesel power has been limited, resulting in part from a measure of technological backwardness and in part from the cost of possibly imported diesel fuel relative to locally mined coal. In a race to modernize their countries, many Third World nations bought diesel locomotives, but found that spares, skilled labour and other factors meant that such locomotives were not the bargain these countries thought they should have been. Nevertheless, many countries without their own locomotive manufacturing capability relied heavily on the import of engines, largely from the United States and the former communist block. In countries such as China and South Africa, however, the growth of diesel traction was limited by the availability of rich reserves of coal and other natural resources, which meant that steam locomotives lingered on much longer than in other places. Important though the introduction of diesel locomotives has been in many countries, it has been the onset of electrification that has had the most dramatic effect on railway operation.

The modern rival to the diesel-powered locomotive for the movement of heavy freight trains, especially in smaller countries such as the U.K. in which it was a relatively straightforward task to adapt the whole of the network within a reasonable

Swindon plant created six classes of diesel-hydraulic locomotives built to the extent of more than 300 units. All of these had been retired by 1977 as their maintenance requirements were too heavy. Some of the diesel-electric designs introduced by British Railways, such as the '47' class which first appeared in 1962 and was built to the extent of more than 500 units, are still in service.

The concept of the diesel-powered locomotive took hold in the U.S.S.R. only in World War II, when the country received American-built locomotives of this type. The Soviets then dissected the technical concepts embodied in Alco and Baldwin locomotives and launched themselves on a course of evolutionary development. The Soviets' first type of diesel-electric locomotive was the 'TE1' class that appeared in 1945, and was succeeded from 1953 by an altogether larger 4,000-hp

ABOVE LEFT: The Burlington Pioneer Zephyr route three-car train set from the 1930s. Diesel-electrics for passenger use fell into decline after World War II when they became increasingly used for freight traffic.

LEFT: Union Pacific's 4-4-0 locomotive City of Salina, 1934. The 1970s saw the return of diesel-electric and particularly electric traction following its decline after World War II.

LEFT: A Canadian Pacific freight train leaves the Connaught tunnel in the Canadian Rockies. The building above the portal is the ventilation fan house.

ABOVE: Seattle & North Coast F9-type locomotive at Port Angeles, Washington. The F series was an all-purpose diesel-electric locomotive, built from 1939.

OPPOSITE

ABOVE LEFT: Pitts & Shawmut type 6P-7 H357 freight locomotive.

ABOVE RIGHT: Seattle & North Coast SW-1200-type H56 road switcher locomotive at Port Townsend, Washington.

BELOW LEFT: Bangor & Aroostook type F3 which operated from Bangor in Maine to Aroostook in New Brunswick, Canada.

BELOW RIGHT: Norfolk & Southern diesel-electric No. 6634 at Hammond, Maryland.

Dan Wesson
SHAWMUT LINE
357
SHAWMUT

56

49
BANGOR AND AROOSTOOK
44

6634
NS
NORFOLK SOUTHERN

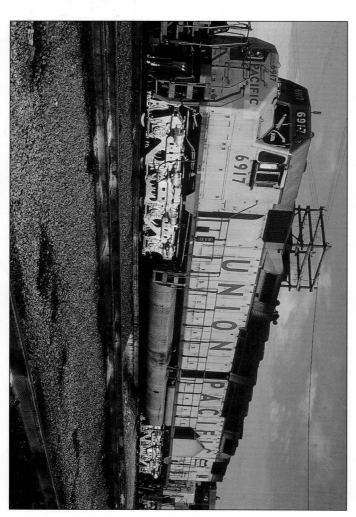

time and at not too exorbitant a cost, is the electrically powered locomotive, which had a higher power/weight ratio and as such may justly be claimed to be a prime example of how the exploitation of modern technology has led to major improvements. The result, as far as railroads are concerned, is the current availability of lightweight locomotives with power outputs far greater than those offered by the giant engines of previous generations. The nature of these locomotives, in the period before the practice of working locomotives in multiple had been developed, meant that the hauling of increasingly heavy trains demanded more traction motors in one machine. This not only increased the locomotive's length and weight, which had to be distributed over several axles, but raised problems of flexibility so that the locomotive could negotiate curves of all but the largest radii.

The locomotives of the so-called 'Frontier Railway', extending from Lulea to Riksgransen in Sweden, provide a good example of the early type of European electric locomotive. The railroad's raison d'être is the high-grade iron ore mined near Kiruna, some 1,670ft (510m) above sea level. Rail was and indeed remains the simplest and most effective way to get the ore to the coast at the port of Narvik in Norway. In 1914 ASEA/Siemens delivered 1-C+C-1 type locomotives each offering 1,800hp (1342kW), but in 1960 the line was using the 'DM3'-class locomotive, a 1+D+D+D-1 giant of 270 tons rated at 9,750hp (7270kW) with an overall length of 82ft 4in (25.0m).

OPPOSITE

LEFT: Type FA locomotive No. 0437 in the snow at Hartford, Connecticut.

RIGHT ABOVE: Norfolk & Western SD-40S freight train in Bluefield West, Virginia.

RIGHT BELOW: A Union Pacific class D D 40AX Centennial at Council Bluffs, built for heavy freight duty.

THIS PAGE

ABOVE: An electric locomotive in a Belgian station. Smaller countries such as Belgium were able to adapt networks for electric running at reasonable costs.

RIGHT: Prototype Belgian diesel locomotive No. 5001. The success of diesel power in America came to influence Europe.

In Switzerland and Austria, the celebrated 'Crocodile' electric locomotives were created specifically to cope with the steep gradients and tight curves of the region's mountainous railroad lines. These 1-C+C-1 type locomotives were so called because the centre cab windows ('eyes') and the sloping machinery compartment ('jaws') suggested that decidedly non-alpine reptile. Switzerland also produced a variety of experimental multi-axle locomotives for the Gotthard route, including a 1-A+A-1-A+A-1+1-A+A-1-A+A-1 that was a remarkable 111ft 6in (34.0m) in length and weighed 604,800lb (274337kg).

The first main-line electrification in North America was on the Camden to Waverley stretch of the Baltimore & Ohio Railroad's system, and it was here that the railroad introduced 1,440-hp (1074-kW) locomotives turning the scales at 215,040lb (97542kg) and able to haul a 1,870-ton train. The Pennsylvania Railroad, the largest electric operator among the main operators, used the renowned sleek and powerful dual-voltage 'GG1'-class units, which ran passenger services between New York and Washington D.C. These 2-Co+Co-2 machines weighed 515,200lb (233694kg), were 79ft 6in (24.23m) long and had a continuous rating of 4,260hp (3176kW). The Virginia Railroad introduced 30 'Triplex' 1-B-B-1+1-B-1+1-BB-1 locomotives 152ft (46m) long and capable of handling trains of 5,350 tons on 1/50 gradients between Mullens and Roanoke.

Japan had some powerful Bo+Bo+Bo-Bo machines on its Tokaido line, but one of the

high points of electric locomotive capability in the 3ft 6in (1.067m) gauge fell to South Africa, where three '3E' 1,200-hp (895-kW) locomotives, working in multiple, hauled 1,500-ton trains from 2,210ft (675m) to 4,980ft (1520m) on the line linking Pietermaritzburg and Glencoe. Such was the pace of development, though, that by the 1980s three '9E' class 5,070-hp (3780-kW) locomotives built by GEC of England and working in multiple, were handling 20,000-ton coal trains on 1/250 gradients.

The 200 miles (322km) of electrified route eastward out of the Indian port of Bombay is notable for some very steep gradients in the Ghats on the route to Igatpuri. In 1925 the railroad received C+C locomotives weighing 268,800lb (121928kg) and producing 2,100hp (1566kW) together with 2-Co-1 and 2-Co-2 passenger machines with a tractive effort of 33,600lb (15241kg), but in 1951 it was able to start replacing these earlier locomotives as it took delivery of its first Co+Co machines each weighing 275,520lb (124976kg) and providing a tractive effort of 75,000lb (34020kg).

In the U.S.S.R: (now Commonwealth of Independent States), the Siberian part of Russia east of the Ural mountains can boast the largest locomotive in the Asian continent. This 'WL-86' class double Bo+Bo+Bo unit is 147ft 6in (45.0m) long and weighs 671,958lb (304800kg), and is operated on the section of the Trans-Siberian Railway connecting Lake Baikal and the Amur river. Built at Novocherkassk in 1985/6, this unit develops 15,287hp (11398kW) and is capable of 100mph (161km/h).

Switzerland has often pioneered the effective use of modern railroad technology. This fact is as true today as it ever was, as indicated by the '465' class of Bo-Bo locomotives each weighing a mere 180,776lb (82000kg) but providing a one-hour power rating of nearly 9,400hp (7009kW). In July 1996 two similar '460' and two '465'-class engines, positioned in a 3,212-ton freight train, lifted it over the 1/37 gradient of the Lötschberg at speeds on the climb ranging from 31 to 43mph (50 to 70km/h) – all in all, a truly prodigious performance.

OPPOSITE
ABOVE: An English Electric Type 3 trundles under a bridge with a train of empty hoppers heading south towards London.

BELOW: Modern freight trains can deliver raw materials to the very heart of industry.

THIS PAGE
ABOVE: China's coal-train network is highly developed. Here a double-headed train wends its way to Gantang.

RIGHT: Union Pacific locomotive No. 6936 B with mixed freight and passenger trains.

Picture Acknowledgements

*Association of American Railroads: page 52 top
*Atchison, Topeka & Santa Fe Railway: page 26 top
*Austrian State Railways: pages 54 top, 55 top right
*Baltimore & Ohio Railroad Museum: pages 16 below, 23 right, 31 top, 38 second left, 39 below, 48 top right
*BBC Hulton Picture Library, London: page 13 left
*British Rail: page 51 below left
British Transport Films, London: page 28 top
*Burlington Northern Railroad: pages 28 below right, 37 top right
*Canadian National Railway: page 30
*Canadian Pacific Railway: page 58 left
*Denver & Rio Grande Railroad: page 32 below
*Deutsche Bundesbahn: page 43 all
*EFf Bahn, Burgdorf: page 55 above right
*Finnish State Railways: pages 40 right, 44
*Freightliner Ltd.: pages 38 far left, 38 third left
*Friedrich Krupp GmbH, Duisburg: page 39 top
*General Electric Company: page 54 below
*Germany: page 39 top
*Illinois Central Railroad: page 51 below right
Image Select, London, © Andrew Rapacz: page 41
*Italian State Railways, Rome: page 10 both
Military Archives & Research Services, Lincolnshire, England: pages 16 top left, 23 left, 26 below, 37 top left, 48 top left, 48 below left and right, 50 above, 51 top left and right, 52 below, 55 below left and right, 56 both, 57 top left and right, 60 all, 61 both, 62 both
*Missouri Pacific Railroad: page 9 right
*Norfolk & Western Railway Co., Virginia: page 28 below left
*Northern Pacific Railroad: pages 8, 9 left
©P.B. Whitehouse: pages 11 all, 12 both, 13 right, above and below, 14 right, 15 both, 46
*Portuguese State Railways: pages 24 below left and right, 25 top left and right
Quebec Cartier Mining Co.: transparency from the J.G. Moore Collection: page 31 below
©Railfotos, Millbrook House Limited, Oldbury, W. Midlands, England: title pages, 14 left, 16 top right, 17 both, 18, 19 both, 20, 21, 24 top, 25 below, 29, 32 top, 33, 34, 35 top, 36, 38 above, 40 left, 42, 47 both, 63 both
*Santa Fe Railway: print from the J.G. Moore Collection: page 49 top
*Union Pacific Railroad: print from the J.G. Moore Collection: pages 4-5, 7
*Union Pacific Railroad Museum: page 27 below, 49 below, 53, 57 below
*U.S. Library of Congress: page 6
*Westrail, Perth: page 35 below
York Trailer: page 37 below left

* Print/transparency through Military Archives & Research Services, Lincolnshire, England.